MW00779364

Taking Off Roofs and Building Bridges

Taking Off Roofs and Building Bridges

Worldview Apologetics for Assessing and Critiquing Systems of Belief

Alan J. Pihringer

RESOURCE *Publications* · Eugene, Oregon

TAKING OFF ROOFS AND BUILDING BRIDGES
Worldview Apologetics for Assessing and Critiquing Systems of Belief

Copyright © 2022 Alan J. Pihringer. All rights reserved. Except for brief quotations in critical publications or reviews, no part of this book may be reproduced in any manner without prior written permission from the publisher. Write: Permissions, Wipf and Stock Publishers, 199 W. 8th Ave., Suite 3, Eugene, OR 97401.

Resource Publications
An Imprint of Wipf and Stock Publishers
199 W. 8th Ave., Suite 3
Eugene, OR 97401

www.wipfandstock.com

PAPERBACK ISBN: 978-1-6667-3386-0
HARDCOVER ISBN: 978-1-6667-2884-2
EBOOK ISBN: 978-1-6667-2885-9

09/26/22

This book is lovingly dedicated to Trisha Pihringer, my wife, friend, and partner in life for many years. You have challenged me and encouraged me and always stood by my side. God has used you as a mighty tool in forming me into the man I am today. I would not be where I am or who I am without you. Thank you for loving me.

"Unfortunately, in this world of ours, each person views things through a certain medium, and so is prevented from seeing in the same light as others."

—ALEXANDRE DUMAS,
The Count of Monte Cristo

Contents

Introduction

I SAT ACROSS FROM a very handsome, young Indian couple in my church office. Our church, although small, was on a busy street, and they happened upon it in their drive. They stopped at the office and asked to speak with the pastor, which I was all too eager to accommodate—God gave a divine appointment for me to share the good news and for them to hear gospel truths. I would not waste that opportunity. I led them into my office, had them sit on the not-so-comfortable couch, and asked them what led them to stop by our little church. They answered simply and matter-of-factly, "We want to get married." As a pastor, I have often been asked to perform weddings, but never from someone who just walked in off the street. I was confused and intrigued at the same time.

Since I hold to a solid biblical view of marriage, I generally do not perform weddings for just anybody. I will only conduct a ceremony for two Christians who agree with the biblical stance on marriage. I asked them about themselves and their background. Their families immigrated to America, and the two met and fell in love. They both had good jobs and good family relations. When I asked them about their religious beliefs, they replied that they were Hindu and were occasionally involved in a local Hindu temple, but they were not overly religious. When I asked why they wanted a Baptist pastor to perform the wedding ceremony, they were very vague, but it seemed that it would take some time to get married at the Hindu temple. If I understood the subtext to what they were saying, they assumed that any pastor at any church would perform a wedding ceremony on a whim because it was part of their job. Bank tellers deposit money. Police arrest bad people. Firefighters put out fires. Pastors perform weddings. That is the way the world works.

Given the subject, I thought there could be no better way to introduce the gospel than by describing the picture marriage gives of Christ and his church. I explained that Christians hold marriage as sacred because it is not only a lifelong commitment but paints a beautiful picture of Jesus Christ, the bridegroom, sacrificing himself for his bride, the Church. I explained the gospel message, expounding on the Christian understanding of God, sin, and the redemption bought by Christ's death that offers us eternal life. I pontificated on the resurrection of Christ, who then ascended into heaven and rules and reigns forever. God gave me such a grand opportunity; I was not going to squander the chance to lead this beautiful couple to Christ. I gave a lot of information in a short amount of time. I asked them what they thought about what I shared and if they would want to follow Jesus Christ. I expected (in my pride) that they would joyfully become disciples of Jesus Christ, and I would get the chance to guide and disciple them. Instead, I was met with silent stares. By the way they were looking at me, I expected the proverbial cricket sounds. They did not understand one word I said.

They did not repent and believe in Jesus that day. And I did not perform a wedding. I gave them my information but never heard from them again. As I pondered upon the encounter, I wondered about the seeming gap in communication. They did not understand what I was saying. I gave the information in (what I thought was) easy, everyday language. I did not use 'Christianese' to explain the good news. Yet, the truth still did not seem to penetrate through whatever barrier was there. It was not until I would later do my studies in apologetics that I realized the obstacle I did not consider that day. The young couple and I had differing worldviews that looked at the world from different contexts. The difference between a Christian worldview and other worldviews cannot be likened to how apples and oranges are different—they have different colors and tastes but are both roundish fruits, so at least they have some things in common. It is more like how Einstein and a bag of rocks are different—there is very little commonality. When sharing the Christian faith or defending the Christian faith, those differences must be considered and overcome.

Everyone has a worldview—a belief system, a set of presuppositions that informs how one looks at, interprets, and interacts with the world. A person tackles the most critical issues of life through one's worldview, be it something as profound as the origin of the universe or something more personal like one's view of marriage. Worldview is the filter that guides one's decisions and determines the course of life. Although every person is unique, people can hold a common worldview. Yet the varied worldviews themselves answer life's important questions in different, often contradictory, ways. Since they contradict one another, they cannot all be true. That being the case, there must be a way of comparing and contrasting worldviews and determining their correspondence to the truth. This, I believe, is the place of Christian apologetics.

Francis Schaeffer likened apologetics to taking the roof off.[1] Taking the roof off refers to exposing the weaknesses and inconsistencies in a false worldview. But it is not enough merely to demonstrate why a worldview is wrong; it is essential to then build a bridge for that person to the one true worldview, Christianity. This book discusses an apologetic method of analyzing, engaging, and critiquing worldviews that will both take the roof off and build a bridge.

Chapter 1 considers why another way or method of apologetics is needed. Different eras raise different challenges to the Christian faith and must be met with tools that Christians can use for defense, analysis, and critique. After a brief historical survey on how this has held true throughout church history, I introduce the foundation of this particular method and why it benefits the current cultural atmosphere worldwide.

Chapter 2 discusses the history of worldview as a concept in Christian thought and how the Christian apologetic task has encompassed the notion. I consider a diverse series of scholarship regarding worldview analysis and recognize the remarkable contributions of several of its advocates. I include careful consideration of what worldview means within the scope of this apologetic, for as Douglas Wilson warns, "The use of popular words like 'worldview' is always dangerous. As words enter into common currency, they can soon cease to be helpful as they become 'buzzwords'—words that evoke a certain response but still remain nebulous and undefined."[2]

Chapter 3 considers the use of abductive reasoning—inference to the best explanation—in philosophical discussions generally and Christian apologetics specifically. It will examine the strengths and weaknesses of

---

1. See Schaeffer, *God Who Is There*, 140–42.
2. Wilson, *The Paideia of God*, 130–31.

this form of logic in discovering the truth, including consideration of how abductive reasoning fits within the scope of testing worldview claims.

Chapter 4 begins the proper consideration of the philosophical groundwork for testing the truthfulness of competing worldviews. Specific foundational epistemological theories of truth undergird this apologetic. While much debate has occurred between adherents of the various approaches (pitting one approach against another), I find that together they make a cumulative test for truthfulness that is best able to abductively analyze the truth claims of the various worldviews. While some contemporary apologists often deal with just two of these theories (coherence and correspondence), the third theory of pragmatism also undergirds the basis of these particular tests. Thus, the coherence theory would cause one to test the logical consistency of a worldview claim, the correspondence theory would cause one to test the empirical adequacy of a worldview claim, and finally, the pragmatic theory would cause one to test the livability or experiential relevance of a worldview claim. Norm Geisler notes that there are rare cases in which the pantheistic worldview may seemingly pass these tests and still be false. In such cases, he added other tests: the undeniability test and the unaffirmability test. This chapter demonstrates how the epistemological theories and the tests that they birth give a strong probability of finding the truth and falsity of worldviews. Or, put another way, how they tear the roofs off other worldviews, providing an opportunity to build a bridge to the Christian worldview.

Chapter 5 considers the four life questions that give the context within which these truth tests analyze the various worldviews. How worldviews give their answers within the subjects of the origin of life, meaning, morality, and destiny determines if their worldview gives a coherent system that corresponds with reality and is livable. These four questions appear broad, but most of the essential questions about existence in this universe fall within one (or possibly more) of these categories. The chapter will then describe and critique how apologists utilize the tests for truth within the areas of the four basic life questions to analyze the major categories of worldviews. Worldview apologists demonstrate how naturalistic humanism, Islam, and Hinduism fail truth standards, while those same tests validate Christian truth claims. Even though those four systems are by no means exhaustive of the plethora of worldviews, it demonstrates how one can use the apologetic for testing almost every classification of worldview, be it atheistic, theistic, or pantheistic.

Chapter 6 brings the work to a close with a challenge to not merely view worldview apologetics as an academic exercise but that it would be a tool in the hands of a Christian to cause another to reflect on their presuppositions deeply and to build a bridge to serious consideration of the gospel of Jesus Christ and the truthfulness of the Christian worldview.

While most of this work takes a scholarly approach, I hope that any individual from any background would find valuable tools and information to equip them to defend the Christian faith and engage other belief systems.

1

Rising to the Challenge

Why Another Approach?

"If Christianity was something we were making up, of course we could make it easier. But it is not. We cannot compete, in simplicity, with people who are inventing religions. How could we? We are dealing with Fact. Of course anyone can be simple if he has no facts to bother about."

—C.S. LEWIS, *Mere Christianity*

CHRISTIAN APOLOGETICS (VERY SIMPLY, the defense of the doctrines and beliefs of the Christian religion) has given strength to the weary Christian, challenged the most vigorous critic, and fed intellectual nourishment to the curious seeker since the very inception of the faith. Disputes against the claims and teachings of Jesus arose from the early days of his earthly ministry and have demonstrated no signs of diminishing in the near two-thousand years since. That being the case, apologetic approaches and methodologies in various forms developed over Christianity's long history to meet the contemporary debates and arguments that contended against the truthfulness and legitimacy of belief in God, Christ, and the body of faith that developed from the traditions handed down by their adherents. Approaches then also developed that would challenge the foundations of the opposing philosophies and religions.

With the dawning of the twenty-first century, new challenges, attacks, and barriers to the faith (and to the apologetic task itself) constantly and consistently arise, coming alongside some of the same contentions from millennia ago. There are, of course, the usual religious and philosophical challenges to the Christian faith, denying the tenets of our statements of belief or the entire system itself. Hinduism and Islam, among other religions and philosophies, still claim to be the genuine way of peace and hope. At the same time, secularistic atheists seek to minimize (if not entirely extinguish) any semblance of Christian influence, declaring the world has moved on from such myths and pronouncing that religion has been the cause of most of the world's ills. They have used inflammatory rhetoric to lay at the feet of religion in general, and Christianity in particular, the blame for most of society's problems. For example, Christopher Hitchens warns his readers, "People of faith are in their different ways planning your and my destruction, and the destruction of all the hard-won human attainments that I have touched upon. *Religion poisons everything*."[1] His fellow 'Horseman of the New Atheism,' Sam Harris, also chimes in, stating, "Religion is to be credited as much for wars of conquest as for feast days and brotherly love. . . . The proportion of abuses for which religion could be found directly responsible is likely to remain undiminished."[2]

In the past few centuries, newer attacks have attempted to undermine the foundations of what both religious and secular thinkers have generally accepted about truth and reality (which would then undercut the very purpose of apologetics and any claims of knowing and demonstrating the truth). For instance, the atmosphere within academic and cultural groups has become caustic toward any claim of exclusive truth, much less the Christian claim. We live in a time when you can philosophically, morally, and religiously believe anything you want as long as you do not claim your beliefs alone are true. And any mention of the exclusivity of Christ seems to bring even greater ire than any other claim. The contemporary representatives of such truth-skeptics, the postmodernists, denounce the claim that one truth applies to everyone since all people are free to create reality for themselves. Of course, the concept of postmodernism itself is very fluid. Brendan Sweetman gives a helpful summary to define the postmodern concept when he describes postmodernism as a "movement whose central theme is the critique of objective rationality and identity, and the working

1. Hitchens, *God Is Not* Great, 13. Emphasis original.
2. Harris, *The End of Faith*, 25.

out of the implications of this critique for the central questions in philosophy, literature, and culture."[3] It makes one wonder why anyone should take their critiques and concepts as objectively true or rational if there is no objective truth or rationality.

In addition, there are the pluralists who deem it arrogant to claim that there is only one way to God and one way to truth. In a debate between Christopher Hitchens and Rabbi David J. Wolpe, Hitchens proclaims, "By what right, rabbi, do you say that you know God better than [nonbelievers] do, that your God is better than theirs, that you have an access that I can't claim to have, to knowing not just that there is a God, but that you know his mind. You put it modestly, but it is a fantastically arrogant claim that you make—an incredibly immodest claim."[4] Thus, any defense of an exclusive faith and an exclusive claim to the truth already meets barriers to its use, much less to the message it seeks to protect and convey.

Piggybacking on the philosophies of postmodernism and pluralism come challenges to the viability of the apologetic task itself. There is a growing contingent on the fringes of Christian evangelicalism that views the apologetic endeavor as tainted by Enlightenment thinking which places man's reason as the absolute authority. These pseudo-evangelicals claim that in attempting to establish rational foundations for Christian belief, the apologist uses concepts and words that are far from what genuine Christianity conveyed before the Enlightenment, even undercutting the gospel it aspires to protect.[5] So, instead of putting forth "a set of propositional assertions that can be epistemically justified," in their eyes the defense of the faith is bound up within the life of the individual, where the life lived becomes the apologetic.[6] Consequently, they desire a move from rationality, reasoning, and argumentation to an embodiment—from the propositional to a more personal revelation.[7] Not that anyone would or should deny that a life lived consistently with one's proclaimed faith is essential—it most certainly is. What can be denied, however, is that this somehow impairs an intellectual defense of the faith through evidence and arguments.

Such post-conservatives claim that the Christian apologetic methods of the past several centuries base themselves on a flawed foundationalist

---

3. Sweetman, "Lyotard, Postmodernism, and Religion," 139–40.

4. Chan, "Hitchens Debates Rabbi Wolpe."

5. Penner, *The End of Apologetics*, 16.

6. Penner, *The End of Apologetics*, 42.

7. Sherman, *Revitalizing Theological Epistemology*, 6.

model that cannot live up to its claims. They maintain that Christianity can stand independently without any form of rational defense, so there is no need to give arguments or provide evidence that Christianity is true and other beliefs are not.[8] They even declare that truth itself is no longer a virtue. Instead, for them, "what matters about truth is that it builds me up, is true for me, and is the kind of thing that connects to my deepest concerns as a self," so, as an alternative to defending the truth, the proper apologetic task entails that "when I witness to a truth that edifies me, I recommend it to someone else as potentially true or edifying for them as well."[9] All these attacks on apologetics come from self-proclaimed Christian theologians who assert that they adhere to an orthodox doctrinal faith that they claim is worthy of academic discussion, only to undermine the truthfulness of their asserted beliefs. Of course, one hopes that the reader has not missed the irony that these authors are attempting to make a reasoned, rational argument for their view that Christian apologetics ought not to use reasoned, rational arguments to commend the faith.

From both 'friend' and foe alike, the twenty-first century has not been kind to the Christian faith or the apologetic task. Still, one cannot overstate the importance of apologetics since it makes way for the gospel message: God will justly and rightly condemn those who do not personally receive the one true faith proclaiming that every man and woman is a sinner separated from God and that Jesus Christ is God the Son who died on the cross and rose again to save said sinners. If the Christian holds to the truthfulness of this belief, then it is imperative to demonstrate these faith-claims in a way that will encourage the non-believer to take serious consideration of Christian assertions and, at the same time, illustrate the falseness of opposing beliefs such that they question those principles to which they wrongly hold. With the gravity of this undertaking, there can be no doubt that how one approaches apologetics is of vital importance, for if the Christian claims are not true in the realm of reality, then there remains no basis for hope.

Based on this eternal significance, the apologetic endeavor exists not only to demonstrate truth (or falsity) to the highest of probabilities but also to open a door for an invitation to personally accept the eternity-changing Christian gospel. As Peter J. Grant reminds Christians, "Apologetics as the handmaiden of evangelism must lead to a clear presentation of the gospel. After all, the only cure for blindness is not information about the *possibility*

8. Sherman, *Revitalizing Theological Epistemology*, 135–36.
9. Penner, *The End of Apologetics*, 111.

of seeing but instead sight itself."[10] Thus, apologetic arguments, evidence, and methods are not the end but the means to the end—although an essential means indeed. Apologetics is not the gospel, but it should clear the barriers to the gospel. However, this view of the place of apologetics in the evangelistic task begs the question: how does one most effectively remove the barriers? Has an apologetic method or procedure arisen for contemporary disputes using a system that effectively demonstrates the truthfulness of Christian claims to a high probability, proves the falseness of contradictory claims, opens the door for a gospel presentation, and even overcomes barriers to using apologetics? Throughout history, Christian apologetic methods arose to meet the varied issues and disputes of the day, and the modern era is no different. To claim an apologetic approach that meets contemporary challenges necessitates a brief survey of how diverse approaches arose in the past in response to conflicts of their day, demonstrating that such a method has emerged for the present.

Progression of Christian Apologetic Approaches

When studying the use of apologetics throughout the history of Christianity, one notices that each era has had an approach that reflected the religious, philosophical, political, and academic atmosphere of the times. As particular challenges surfaced, specific apologetic techniques rose to meet the challenge. It would then be no wonder that such an approach arises in our own day that is more effective than others in managing the modern contentions against the faith. As one set of authors rightly note, "Culture is never stagnant, changing and adapting as ideas evolve, and this means that all apologetics is contextual. Apologetics is a response to culture and its *critiques of* or *questions for* Christianity and is always done in conversation with culture and the people that define it."[11] As the world changes, so do the apologetic methods.

In surveying the history of apologetics, we notice that varied approaches have come and gone. Still, they met their opposition with effectiveness and enthusiasm, which gives hope for a contemporary approach to do the same. It is helpful to consider how apologists who have come before confronted the issues of their times to inform the present on how better to face the issues of the modern day. The methods and systems of

10. Grant, "The Priority of Apologetics," 65. Emphasis original.

11. Forrest et al., *The History of Apologetics*, 23. Emphasis original.

past apologetics often evolved themselves with the times and new challenges that arose. As William Edgar and K. Scott Oliphint state, "While the intellectual and social milieus of past authors were different from ours, deep down most of the basic challenges to the faith have been the same. Access to both historical and contemporary texts gives us fresh insight into how our fathers in the faith responded to the questions facing them. We thus can learn from their strengths and weaknesses. Reading them can also better inform us about how to be 'in the world but not of it.' The great apologists, in varying degrees and with various postures, found themselves using the language of the day without wanting to succumb to the basic systems behind that language."[12] The modern task is similar in that apologists seek an approach that meets the questions of the day using the language of the day without succumbing to the spirit of the day. Thus, gleaning insight from the past will inform the practice of the present.

The founders of the faith practiced apologetics to defend 'the Way' against the resistance of those holding to a form of godliness and religion but denying its power (2 Tim 3:5). Jesus himself utilized many of the tools often associated with mounting a defense against detractors. As Douglas Groothuis and Sean McDowell demonstrate from the Gospel accounts, Jesus defended his teachings and claims using logical argumentative techniques such as reductio ad absurdum and a fortiori arguments, as well as by making appeals to observable and verifiable evidence such as eyewitness testimony and miracles.[13] The apostle Paul also used reasoned arguments and proofs demonstrating the veracity of the Christian faith. Acts 9:22 describes Paul as having "confounded" the Jews by "proving" the truths of Jesus' identity.[14] Acts 17:17 describes Paul as having "reasoned" every day with those he would meet in the synagogue or the marketplace. Acts 19:8 describes Paul as "reasoning" and "persuading," and in Acts 19:9, Paul was "reasoning daily" with the Jews. In Philippians 1:7, Paul describes his ministry as a "defense and confirmation of the gospel." Therefore, from this small survey, I contend that the apologetic endeavor is biblical and foundational to Christian ministry.

12. Edgar and Oliphint, *Apologetics Past and Present*, 1:6.

13. Groothuis, "Jesus: Philosopher and Apologist;" McDowell, "Was Jesus an Apologist?"

14. Unless otherwise noted, all Scripture quotations and references are from the English Standard Version.

After the founding of the faith, there was a bitter antagonism to the teachings of the fledgling church stemming from the Jews, the pagans, and the false teachers. The apostles and biblical writers as apologists came with reasoned defenses to meet the hostility directly and to open doors to the presentation of the gospel. Rational and empirical evidence lent support to the message of Christ that Scripture would subsequently record since, as John Warwick Montgomery postulates, "The Bible, unlike the Qur'an and the 'holy books' of other religions, does not expect its readers to accept its revelational character simply because the text claims to be true."[15] These apologies of the apostles and biblical authors came in several forms.

First, the biblical authors frequently noted that the content of their writing emanated from eyewitness testimony (either their own or someone with whom they had discourse); therefore, the events they record are historically accurate and verifiably true. The author Luke in Luke 1:1–4 wrote that he undertook the task of compiling an accurate narrative of the life of Christ based on eyewitness testimony so that the intended readers would be confident of Christian teachings. The apostle John in 1 John 1:1–3 described the teachings in his epistle as based on what he and the other apostles saw with their own eyes and touched with their own hands. The apostle Peter confirmed in 2 Peter 1:16 that he and the other apostles were not pandering some myth, but their teachings were historically accurate, and therefore true because of their basis on the eyewitness accounts of countless people. Even the apostle Paul, as mentioned earlier, argued and reasoned with others that they could know the truthfulness of his claims, especially that of the resurrection of Christ, due to hundreds of eyewitnesses (1 Cor 15:4–8).

Second, the biblical authors established the truthfulness of Christian faith-claims by revealing the fulfillment of Old Testament prophecy—how the scriptural texts foretold and prefigured the life, death, and resurrection of Jesus Christ—continuing God's plan for redemptive history. So, in putting forth their interpretation of the ancient texts, the biblical authors gave their arguments with "the growing insistence that every detail unfolds 'as it was written.'"[16] The gospel of Matthew alone indicates thirteen times that certain events in Jesus' life occur in fulfillment of certain words and prophecies given by the Old Testament prophets, but Matthew is not alone. Harry L. Poe notes that the "idea of the fulfillment of [Old Testament]

---

15. Montgomery, "Short History of Apologetics," 21.

16. Dulles, *A History of Apologetics*, 6.

Scripture [by Christ] appears in every book of the New Testament except James."[17] To dismiss this particular line of evidence due to one's presumption that no such thing is possible places upon that person the burden to put forward alternative explanations, for the fact that the biblical authors wrote these prophecies before the life of Jesus is undeniable, and the fact that he fulfilled them is quite evident. Thus, the apostles and early church leaders sought to exhibit the message's credibility and answer objections they met during their ministries so there would be no barriers to a pure gospel message.

At the turn of the first century, "apologetics became the most characteristic form of Christian writing."[18] However, the reasoned defense went further than merely establishing credibility. Christianity became an unwelcomed religion in the Roman Empire and faced several fronts upon which to defend the faith—persecution from without (stemming from such misconceived charges as atheism and immorality and cannibalism), heresy within, and worldview conflict all around. The apologetic methodology focused on refuting charges, rebutting falsehoods, gaining civil tolerance with governmental authorities, and winning new converts to the faith.[19] The apologists again pointed to the many Old Testament prophecies fulfilled in Christ and the evidence of miracles in his ministry (with the resurrection being the greatest of the miracles).[20] They also aggressively defended the faith to the civil authorities (often writing to the Emperor himself) to gain tolerance. Their writings demonstrated that Christianity had an exalted view of God (considering the faith a more fulfilled form of philosophy) and argued that Christians were not guilty of the misconstrued charges against them. They wanted authorities to know that there was nothing in Christianity that was criminal or detrimental to the State—if anything, Christians ought to have made some of the best citizens within the Empire.[21] For example, Justin Martyr argues that Christians know to act rightly since they understand God is always watching their actions. Christians will always be faithful in fulfilling their civil obligation (that do not contradict Scripture) in such things as paying taxes seeing as Christ himself so directed (Matthew

17. Poe, *Gospel and Its Meaning*, 83.

18. Dulles, *A History of Apologetics*, 27.

19. Dulles, *A History of Apologetics*, 28.

20. Montgomery, "Short History of Apologetics," 22.

21. Dulles, *A History of Apologetics*, 36.

22:20–21).[22] Martyr aptly balanced philosophy and divine revelation for his defense, paving the way for future apologists.

The apologies of the time were not merely defensive but also went on the offensive against pagan beliefs, Gnosticism, and rising heresies within the ranks of Christianity itself. Apologists argued that pagans were the real atheists since they worshipped objects that were not divine. Their religion did not lead to a good life loyal to the civil authorities (unlike Christianity).[23] For example, Tertullian argued that pagan gods did not exist, and even in their stories they are presented as no more than glorified men. He writes,

> We do not worship your gods, because we know that there are no such beings. This, therefore, is what you should do: you should call on us to demonstrate their non-existence, and thereby prove that they have no claim to adoration; for only if your gods were truly so, would there be any obligation to render divine homage to them. And punishment even were due to Christians, if it were made plain that those to whom they refused all worship were indeed divine. But you say, They are gods. We protest and appeal from yourselves to your knowledge; let that judge us; let that condemn us, if it can deny that all these gods of yours were but men. If even it venture to deny that, it will be confuted by its own books of antiquities, from which it has got its information about them, bearing witness to this day, as they plainly do, both of the cities in which they were born, and the countries in which they have left traces of their exploits, as well as where also they are proved to have been buried.[24]

Tertullian's apologetic approach to the pagans emphasized morality— their crude pagan gods were immoral, leading to corrupt human practices. However, the Christian God was pure and holy, leading to good and just human practices.[25]

Apologists would then battle heresies such as Gnosticism and Arianism by giving a thorough, systematized account of true, biblical, orthodox Christianity. For example, Irenaeus accuses Gnostics of twisting Scripture to suit their purposes, writing, "Then, again, collecting a set of expressions and names scattered here and there [in Scripture], they twist them, as we have already said, from a natural to a non-natural sense. In so doing, they

22. See Martyr, "First Apology," chapters 11–17.

23. Edgar and Oliphint, *Apologetics Past and Present*, 1:117.

24. Tertullian, *The Apology*, chapter 10.

25. Litfin, "Tertullian of Carthage," 91.

act like those who bring forward any kind of hypothesis they fancy, and then endeavor to support them out of the poems of Homer, so that the ignorant imagine that Homer actually composed the verses bearing upon that hypothesis, which has, in fact, been but newly constructed; and many others are led so far by the regularly-formed sequence of the verses, as to doubt whether Homer may not have composed them."[26] Irenaeus, to contrast the theological perversions of the Gnostics, then goes on to succinctly summarize the true theology of the Christian faith handed down to all the saints, explaining,

> The Church, though dispersed throughout the whole world, even to the ends of the earth, has received from the apostles and their disciples this faith: [She believes] in one God, the Father Almighty, Maker of heaven, and earth, and the sea, and all things that are in them; and in one Christ Jesus, the Son of God, who became incarnate for our salvation; and in the Holy Spirit, who proclaimed through the prophets the dispensations of God, and the advents, and the birth from a virgin, and the passion, and the resurrection from the dead, and the ascension into heaven in the flesh of the beloved Christ Jesus, our Lord, and His [future] manifestation from heaven in the glory of the Father "to gather all things in one," and to raise up anew all flesh of the whole human race, in order that to Christ Jesus, our Lord, and God, and Savior, and King, according to the will of the invisible Father, "every knee should bow, of things in heaven, and things in earth, and things under the earth, and that every tongue should confess" to Him, and that He should execute just judgment towards all; that He may send "spiritual wickednesses," and the angels who transgressed and became apostates, together with the ungodly, and unrighteous, and wicked, and profane among men, into everlasting fire; but may, in the exercise of His grace, confer immortality on the righteous, and holy, and those who have kept His commandments, and have persevered in His love, some from the beginning [of their Christian course], and others from [the date of] their repentance, and may surround them with everlasting glory.[27]

Irenaeus was unique in that while most apologists of his time drew upon philosophical arguments that were common for the time, he instead utilized rhetorical strategies including hypothesis, dispensation, and

---

26. Irenaeus, "Against Heresies," 1.9.1
27. Irenaeus, "Against Heresies," 1.10.1.

recapitulation.[28] While fighting the same battles, the apologists used techniques based on the tools they had at the moment and would meet the need for the particular objections. So, Irenaeus' methods included "a basic pattern for analyzing heretical perspectives, using questions and dilemma, parody, critiquing their sources, and critiquing their immorality."[29] These were the tools he found useful to demonstrate the falsehood of the Gnostics. His method took form based on his contemporary situation and circumstances—the pattern for Christian apologetics throughout its history.

As the patristic period closed, apologists began integrating philosophic knowledge with traditional Christian teachings to establish Christianity within a more extensive metaphysical system.[30] Augustine used epistemological argumentation to defend the ability to obtain certain knowledge against the skeptics, of which he was formerly an adherent. (Epistemology is the philosophical study of knowledge.) For Augustine, Christianity was an entire worldview that was knowable and livable. He then consolidated the tools of previous apologists to lay the groundwork of belief and blazed a trail of influence for centuries to follow.[31] As an example of his epistemic moorings, in a passage that seems a precursor to Descartes' famous quip, he writes:

> [W]ithout any delusive representation of images or phantasms, I am most certain that I am, and that I know and delight in this. In respect of these truths, I am not at all afraid of the arguments of the Academicians, who say, What if you are deceived? For if I am deceived, I am. For he who is not, cannot be deceived; and if I am deceived, by this same token I am. And since I am if I am deceived, how am I deceived in believing that I am? for it is certain that I am if I am deceived. Since, therefore, I, the person deceived, should be, even if I were deceived, certainly I am not deceived in this knowledge that I am. And, consequently, neither am I deceived in knowing that I know. For, as I know that I am, so I know this also, that I know.[32]

For Augustine, specific knowledge is knowable. Not only is knowledge possible, but truth itself is knowable, for it is eternal. As Augustine and his "Reason" interact about the subject, he writes,

---

28. Presley, "Irenaeus of Lyons," 56–57.
29. Presley, "Irenaeus of Lyons," 61.
30. Edgar and Oliphint, *Apologetics Past and Present*, 1:205.
31. Frame, *History of Western Philosophy*, 108.
32. Augustine, "The City of God," 11.26.1.

R. Furthermore, does it seem to you that anything can be true, and
not be Truth?

A. In no wise.

R. There will therefore be Truth, even though the frame of things
should pass away.

A. I cannot deny it.

R. What if Truth herself should perish? will it not be true that
Truth has perished?

A. And even that who can deny?

R. But that which is true cannot be, if Truth is not.

A. I have just conceded this.

R. In no wise therefore can Truth fail.

A. Proceed as thou hast begun, for than this deduction nothing is
truer.[33]

Therefore, the truths of the Christian worldview (the Christian metaphysical system) are knowable and defendable and are arguably the only
certain and necessary truths that exist. When someone believes and lives in
the truth of the Christian worldview, it sets them apart from the rest of the
world and all of its various belief systems. There is an antithesis between the
Christian worldview and all others—one living in truth and pure knowledge, the other living in vanity. For Augustine, one is the City of God, and all
others are the Earthly City. He explains, "Accordingly, two cities have been
formed by two loves: the earthly by the love of self, even to the contempt
of God; the heavenly by the love of God, even to the contempt of self. The
former, in a word, glories in itself, the latter in the Lord."[34] For Augustine,
only the Christian worldview offered truth and wisdom and knowledge.

While persecution and problems for Christians intensified toward
the end of the third century, the political landscape of the empire changed
during the fourth century, bringing with it a change in the status of Christianity in the public realm. With the Edict of Toleration by Galerius and
then the Edict of Milan by Constantine and Licinius, Christianity gained
a position of legitimacy and received toleration that it did not previously
enjoy. Not only did this alleviate much of the pressure Christianity had
suffered, but it would alter how the apologists practiced their task over the
next several centuries.[35] Apologists would still battle against the beliefs of
non-Christians (such as the invading barbarians, the unconverted Jews, and

33. Augustine, "Soliloquies," 2.2.2.

34. Augustine, "The City of God," 14.28.1.

35. Edgar and Oliphint, *Apologetics Past and Present*, 1:312.

the growing power of Islam) while at the same time ingratiating the true doctrine of the one true faith to them for the sake of their conversions.[36] For example, John Chrysostom wrote a discourse to prove to pagans that Christ is God by referring to Christ's historicity, Christ's fulfillment of Old Testament prophecy, the fulfillment of Christ's prophecies about the destruction of the Jewish temple, and the miraculous growth of the church even amid persecution.[37] The new openness with which they could practice and live the Christian faith freed apologists and theologians to seek a deeper understanding of the faith handed down to them through the centuries. This freedom led to establishing schools and universities to further propagate the Christian faith.

With the liberty to pursue scholarship and academics, discussions ensued regarding the relationship between faith and reason within religious life and work which directly affected the apologetic task. Theologians such as Anselm and Augustine believed that reason would bring greater understanding to the faith that one already held—however, reason had limitations in what it could do for those who did not have faith. Anselm demonstrates the delicate balance of faith and reason, stating, "I do not endeavor, O Lord, to penetrate thy sublimity, for in no wise do I compare my understanding with that; but I long to understand in some degree thy truth, which my heart believes and loves. For I do not seek to understand that I may believe, but I believe in order to understand. For this also I believe,—that unless I believed, I should not understand."[38] Anselm may have based his saying on Augustine, who writes, "For understanding is the reward of faith. Therefore do not seek to understand in order to believe, but believe that thou mayest understand."[39] Other theologians and apologists maintained that "human reason, making use of objectively accessible evidence, could achieve some kind of inchoative faith, paving the way for the supernatural act of faith elicited under the influence of grace and charity."[40] This high view of the rational did not necessarily mean that apologists granted reason and philosophy primary status for their purposes. Reason could ingratiate the faith, but faith was in no way a slave to reason. Philosophy was the handmaiden of theology and apologetics, not its lord.

36. Dulles, *A History of Apologetics*, 91.

37. See Chrysostom, "Demonstration against the Pagans."

38. Anselm, *Proslogium*, Chapter 1.

39. Augustine, "Gospel According to St. John," 29.6.

40. Dulles, *A History of Apologetics*, 107.

The most influential apologist of this period was Thomas Aquinas. Aquinas embraced the philosophy of Aristotle and deemed Christian revelation as having corrected and completed Aristotle's teachings—the Christian faith bringing it to greater fulfillment.[41] Aquinas "took over Aristotle's traditional proofs for God's existence and argued that they can establish a foundation of Reason upon which Faith can operate. This stress on the Aristotelian proofs would have a tremendous influence on all subsequent Christian apologetics."[42] Although utilizing Aristotle, Aquinas knew the limitations of reason in ingratiating Christianity to others. Dulles describes the principle behind Aquinas' apology: "The human mind in its effort to discover the divine ground of all things has limited competence. It can establish the existence of the one personal God and many other important religious truths, but there is a higher sphere of truths that remain impenetrable to man unless God is pleased to make them known by revelation."[43] Thus, Aquinas created various arguments that would lead to the conclusion that there was a God: his renowned *Five Ways*, which included the argument from motion, the argument from causality, the argument from contingency, the argument from perfection, and the argument from purpose.[44] However, other truths (such as the Trinity or substitutionary atonement) were only understandable through the special revelation of Scripture.

The cultural manner of the Renaissance followed these Middle Ages with a humanism that returned to and critically examined the primary sources for education, society, and the church.[45] In this atmosphere, the Reformers returned to the original source of authority for the church, the Scriptures, and what they rightly deemed as the original gospel message. Although there was still the aspect of apologetics that reached out and defended the faith against pagan, Jewish, and Islamic beliefs, the apologetics of the era were not so much concerned with doing battle with contrary thoughts outside the faith as much as they were with cleaning up the theology of the medieval church.[46] The defense of the faith became the defense of the nature and authority of the church (Reformed or Roman Catholic): Scripture or the combination of tradition and church. "On the Protestant

---

41. Dulles, *A History of Apologetics*, 113.
42. Montgomery, "Short History of Apologetics," 23.
43. Dulles, *A History of Apologetics*, 115.
44. Thomas Aquinas, *Summa Theologica*, 1 Q 2 a.3.
45. Edgar and Oliphint, *Apologetics Past and Present*, 2:13.
46. Montgomery, "Short History of Apologetics," 23.

side, it was necessary to defend the Reformed religion against its detractors, especially those who thought it was a departure from the true church. . . . Similarly, the Roman Catholic polemicists defended the papacy and the role of tradition against the Protestant approach."[47] For example, as Martin Luther sought to reform the church, he appealed to the Pope that only the true Word of God in the gospel of Christ gives life when accepted by faith, writing, "Let us therefore hold it for certain and firmly established that the soul can do without everything except the word of God, without which none at all of its wants are provided for. . . . But you will ask, What is this word, and by what means is it to be used, since there are so many words of God? I answer, The Apostle Paul (Rom. 1) explains what it is, namely the Gospel of God, concerning His Son, incarnate, suffering, risen, and glorified, through the Spirit, the Sanctifier. To preach Christ is to feed the soul, to justify it, to set it free, and to save it, if it believes the preaching. For faith alone and the efficacious use of the word of God, bring salvation."[48]

In the eighteenth and nineteenth centuries, with the rise of Enlightenment thinking, attacks on Christian claims took on a new force as appeals to the philosophies and sciences of the times sought to label the faith as either mere superstition or at a minimum to strip it of any of its supernatural elements. Secular scholarship grew as academics attempted to assert the independent authority of reason. As the natural sciences found their place, humanity's emphasis on using innate reason in pursuing the truth led to significant discoveries but also led mankind to liberate themselves from God's sovereign claim over His creation. The Enlightenment was a period of great thinking, but it was also a time of great straying, even for supposed Christian leaders. Deism grew throughout Christian circles, which emphasized the natural and held a deep skepticism toward the supernatural. Some, like Lord Herbert of Cherbury, "maintained that revelation was unnecessary because human reason was able to know all the truths requisite for salvation," for, according to him, God had "implanted in the human soul from the beginning five innate religious ideas: the existence of God, divine worship, the practice of virtue, repentance of sin, and personal immortality."[49] This form of religion would evolve such that those who believed in a God disbelieved that he could or would do anything supernatural in the world.

47. Edgar and Oliphint, *Apologetics Past and Present*, 2:17.

48. Luther, *Concerning Christian Liberty*, 364–65.

49. Dulles, "The Deist Minimum," 25; see Herbert, *The Antient Religion of the Gentiles*, 3–4.

Since the world appeared to work according to natural laws, deism believed that God created the world, wound the world up, and let it go without any interference on his part—reason rules, above all else. As deist Thomas Paine said of God, "The only idea that man can affix to the name of God, is that of a first cause, the cause of all things. . . . It is only by the exercise of reason, that man can discover God. Take away that reason, and he would be incapable of understanding any thing."[50]

During this same period, a secular skepticism arose that attempted to deconstruct Christianity to trivialize its claims. David Hume saw little evidence for Christianity, stating, "Our evidence, then, for the truth of the *Christian* religion is less than the evidence for the truth of our senses;" he then flattered himself that he "discovered an argument . . . which, if just, will, with the wise and learned, be an everlasting check to all kinds of superstitious delusion, and consequently, will be useful as long as the world endures. For so long, I presume, will the accounts of miracles and prodigies be found in all history, sacred and profane."[51] Then came the new evolutionary "science" of Charles Darwin, seemingly freeing man from his theological foundations. Complete reliance on reason, science, and nature undermined any reliance on positive historical revelation.

In response to deistic and secular skepticism, "Christian apologetics, seeking to answer in kind, concentrated increasingly on scientific historical evidences and relied rather less upon lofty metaphysical considerations."[52] Some, such as Joseph Butler, would reason that divine revelation (Scripture) did not contradict natural theology. Butler argued that the Deists' natural religion was burdened with the same hindrances they claimed for revealed religion—only demonstrating probability instead of giving complete certainty. Yet, this is an acceptable measure for Butler in consideration of current human circumstances. He writes, "Probable evidence, in its very nature, affords but an imperfect kind of information; and is to be considered as relative only to beings of limited capacities. For nothing which is the possible object of knowledge, whether past, present, or future, can be probable to an infinite Intelligence; since it cannot but be discerned absolutely as it is in itself, certainly true, or certainly false. But to us, probability is the very guide of life."[53] Others, such as William Paley, with his teleological ar-

---

50. Payne, *The Age of Reason*, 27–28.

51. Hume, *Enquiry Concerning Human Understanding*, 114–15. Emphasis original.

52. Dulles, *A History of Apologetics*, 146.

53. Butler, *The Analogy of Religion*, 5.

gument (the argument that design within the natural world demonstrates a Creator), produced rational argumentations that sought to undermine the naturalistic assumptions behind much Enlightenment thinking.[54]

Unfortunately, some, like Friedrich Schleiermacher, attempted to ingratiate the faith to science by compromising Christian beliefs to fit the science of the day and instead struggled to give a defense of the faith via personal experiences of God. Schleiermacher writes,

> Let me say then at once, that the only remaining way for a truly individual religion to arise is to select some one of the great relations of mankind in the world to the Highest Being, and, in a definite way, make it the centre and refer to it all the others. In respect of the idea of religion, this may appear a merely arbitrary proceeding, but, in respect of the peculiarity of the adherents, being the natural expression of their character, it is the purest necessity. Hereby a distinctive spirit and a common character enter the whole at the same time, and the ambiguous and vague reach firm ground. By every formation of this kind one of the endless number of different views and different arrangements of the single elements, which are all possible and all require to be exhibited, is fully realized. Single elements are all seen on the one side that is turned towards this central point, which makes all the feelings have a common tone and a livelier closer interaction.[55]

The rise of this form of Christian liberalism brought with it a criticism that sought to undermine the divine authority of the Bible. Apologists, such as B. B. Warfield, gave reasoned defenses of the faith in general and more specifically to the theological stance of Scriptural inerrancy. While arguing for inspiration specifically and Christianity in general through evidence and arguments, Warfield places everything in their proper perspective, writing, "Inspiration is not the most fundamental of Christian doctrines, nor even the first thing we prove about the Scriptures. It is the last and crowning fact as to the Scriptures. These we first prove authentic, historically credible, generally trustworthy, before we prove them inspired. And the proof of their authenticity, credibility, general trustworthiness would give us a firm basis for Christianity prior to any knowledge on our part of their inspiration, and apart indeed from the existence of inspiration."[56] He and others of the Old Princeton guard provided a place for argumentation

---

54. See Paley, *Natural Theology*, 1–25.

55. Schleiermacher, *On Religion*, 222–23.

56. Warfield, *Revelation and Inspiration*, 210.

and evidence to undergird the truths of inspiration, inerrancy, and other orthodox doctrines. On the other hand, other theologians like Abraham Kuyper believed that the antithesis between believer and unbeliever made it such that one could not merely reason one's way to faith, for there is no point of agreement between the two.[57]

With the dawn of the modern age at the end of the nineteenth century and into the twentieth century (and one could argue into the twenty-first century), apologists emphasized proper methodology.[58] Some still held that reasoned arguments and evidence could sway critics' beliefs. In contrast, others contended that Christians could not communicate rationally with unbelievers due to the noetic effects of sin. Still, others embraced taking a leap of faith, leading to a personal experience with Christ. Cornelius Van Til would take Kuyper's apologetic as a foundation to form his transcendental presuppositionalism, which relied on presupposing the Christian faith to make sense of the world, not argument or evidence.[59] Other Reformed philosophers, like Alvin Plantinga, would also eschew the need for reasoned argumentation to believe. Plantinga came to apologetics from an epistemological standpoint, arguing that a person did not need empirical evidence or deductive arguments to warrant a belief in a God; instead, belief in God was properly basic (although this did not mean that such belief is groundless).[60]

From a more fideistic standpoint, theologians like Søren Kierkegaard and Karl Barth vehemently opposed apologetics since faith alone is superior for one to arrive at the truth. As Barth explains,

> By trying to resist and conquer other religions, we put ourselves on the same level. They, too, appeal to this or that immanent truth in them. They, too, can triumph in the power of the religious self-consciousness, and sometimes they have been astonishingly successful over wide areas. Christianity can take part in this fight. There is no doubt that it does not lack the necessary equipment, and can give a good account of itself alongside the other religions. But do not forget that if it does this it has renounced its birthright. It has renounced the unique power which it has as the religion of revelation. This power dwells only in weakness. And it does not really operate, nor does the power with which Christianity hopes

57. See Abraham Kuyper, *Calvinism*, 29–33.

58. Dulles, *A History of Apologetics*, 353.

59. See Van Til, *The Defense of the Faith*, specifically chapter 6 sections 1 and 2.

60. Plantinga, "Is Belief in God Properly Basic?" 47–48.

to work, the power of religious self-consciousness which is the
gift of grace in the midst of weakness, unless Christianity has first
humbled instead of exalting itself.[61]

Critics often disparage presuppositionalists or reformed epistemologists
for being fideists—eschewing rationality for a mere leap in the dark. To
clarify the distinction, Plantinga defines fideism as the "'exclusive or basic
reliance upon faith alone, accompanied by a consequent disparagement of
reason and utilized especially in the pursuit of philosophical or religious
truth.' Therefore, a fideist urges reliance on faith rather than reason, in
matters philosophical and religious; and he may go on to disparage and
denigrate reason."[62] In contrast, a Reformed epistemologist need not com-
mit to a conflict between faith and reason to explain the proper basicality of
belief, just that there are some central truths to the faith that one may hold
without being based on other reasons or truths.[63] The discussion about
methodology continues without an overall consensus and thus brings this
work to its proper consideration of a way of handling modern contentions
against the faith.

This survey recognizes how apologetic approaches face the different nuances with new times and challenges and acknowledges that there
is much contemporary discussion regarding proper methodology. This
then leads to the question about using an approach toward apologetics for
modern times that defends the truthfulness of Christianity, demonstrates
the falsity of competing religions and philosophies, balks at the cultural
beliefs of postmodernism and relativism, and defeats the challenges to the
apologetic task itself. I find that a more productive discussion first regards
the proper domain wherein to analyze the truth claims of contradictory
systems of thought. Then, after determining this domain, discover tests
that, when applied, determine how one system of thought has a higher
probability of truthfulness over the others.

A Worldview Apologetic Methodology

Over the millennia, many approaches to Christian apologetics have answered contemporary assertions against the faith. The particular issues that
have arisen over the past century again call for an approach that can handle

61. Barth, *Doctrine of the Word*, 332–33.

62. Plantinga, "Reason and Belief," 87.

63. Plantinga, "Reason and Belief," 88–91.

the various religious, philosophical, and cultural concerns. This book contends that testing the veracity of truth-claims from within the scope of entire worldviews is an effective approach to validating Christianity's truthfulness, revealing other worldview's falseness, and neutralizing arguments against the apologetic task itself. The book systematizes, describes, and defends this worldview truth-testing approach, demonstrating its ability to test the truthfulness of all possible worldviews as it weighs the answers the various worldviews give to essential life questions.

To understand this approach, which has developed recently over the past two centuries (often termed "worldview apologetics"), one must apprehend what worldview entails. For example, Ronald Nash states that a worldview "is a conceptual scheme by which we consciously or unconsciously place or fit everything we believe and by which we interpret and judge reality."[64] One's worldview helps one to find meaning, interpret experiences, guide thoughts, and guide actions.[65] The reader can think of a pair of glasses (or contact lenses) through which you might look at the world around you. The glasses or contacts filter how you see things. One interprets the world of ideas, experiences, and purposes through this filter. One bases their decisions through this filter. Now, unlike glasses and contacts, where not everybody needs to wear them, everybody in the world has a worldview. Everybody has a filter through which they interpret reality. However, since people's various worldviews conflict in some way, not all worldviews can be true. Therefore, the apologetic task is to give sound reasons and arguments that show which systems of belief are true or false and why they are so. Every worldview must be tested to determine its correspondence to the truth.

The tests for truth within worldview apologetics base themselves on three epistemological theories of truth working together (where the three may be weak individually, together, they reinforce the truth-testing task): the coherence theory (that the varied claims of the worldview cohere together and follow the known laws of logic); the correspondence theory (where one examines asserted statements to determine their correspondence with reality); and the pragmatic theory (where worldview beliefs are true if they are useful in life and one can logically live out its claims). These theories undergird three tests for the truth that scrutinize each worldview and its implications—this approach tests worldviews for logical

64. Nash, *Worldviews in Conflict*, 16.
65. Holmes, *Contours of a World View*, 3–5.

consistency, empirical adequacy, and experiential relevance. To undergird any weaknesses within these tests, Norm Geisler also considers adding (in some cases) analysis through the unaffirmability and undeniability tests.[66] The apologetic I propose tests for worldview-truthfulness within the context of answering four basic questions of life: origin, meaning, morality, and destiny. So, one considers a worldview's answer to origins and tests to see if it is logically consistent, empirically adequate, and experientially relevant and does the same for all important life-questions. This worldview analysis not only argues for or against particular worldviews but can also be a way for someone to find a worldview to embrace as they seek answers to life's important questions.

Some (such as presuppositionalists, fideists, or postmodernists) may argue that such an apologetic relies too heavily on rationality and gives human reasoning too much autonomy. However, the Christian faith is not antithetical to reason. Christianity is not a blind faith that one embraces despite all the evidence. The Christian worldview is an informed faith— our faith has a basis. Moreover, as noted above, the apostle Paul reasoned and debated with others. Therefore, using argument and persuasion about truth is a biblical concept. Nevertheless, apologists who use philosophical argumentations and empirical evidence will readily admit that the Bible is the ultimate authority, not rational arguments or apologetic methodologies. The use of an apology leads to a hearing of the claims of Scripture, and ultimately, the transformation of a life and the change of a heart is the work of the Holy Spirit through the gospel of Jesus Christ.

Therefore, I consider worldview as the proper field for apologetic engagement. This approach demonstrates that the combined correspondence, coherence, and pragmatic theories are sound considerations for the epistemology of truth when used through abductive reasoning. I will argue that three tests based on these epistemological theories determine truthfulness within strong probability leading one to find a worldview containing all the components of an indisputable life system. I also contend that four questions of life (origin, meaning, morality, and destiny) are the general categories under which most issues of existence fall and where one may compare worldviews for apologetic purposes. I also demonstrate that this approach can interact with different classes of worldviews (such as atheistic, theistic, and pantheistic). Finally, I conclude that this approach is both scholarly

---

66. Geisler, *Christian Apologetics*, 1st Edition, 141. See also Naugle, *Worldview*, 327.

and practical and can overcome the barriers to the apologetic task that have arisen in much contemporary thought and scholarship.

This approach has a significant advantage over single-argument apologetic approaches. David Hume's stopper, which reasons that a sound apologetic argument does not lead to the full-blown Christian conception of God (and, therefore, does not prove enough), has some validity for it would appear to lead to general theism, not necessarily Christianity.[67] Moreover, while a good cumulative case argument for a singular point (e.g., the existence of God) can mitigate such critiques, a cumulative case approach is but one piece of an overall puzzle—that puzzle being an entire worldview.[68] There is no single "smoking gun" argument that leads to a full-fledged Christian theology. Still, with careful epistemological analysis, an apologist can demonstrate the truthfulness of the system as a whole. From a presuppositional or reformed standpoint, this approach can demonstrate why presupposing Christianity as truthful and other worldviews as false has a proper epistemological grounding that the unbeliever's belief system will find hard to deny. It gives a starting point for discussion and debate, which some presuppositionalists might deny exists. It is one thing to assume another worldview is incoherent, but it is another to establish its incoherency in a reasonable fashion.

67. Sennett, "Hume's Stopper and the Natural Theology Project," 82.
68. Geivett, "David Hume and a Cumulative Case Argument," 297–99.

2

What in the World is a Worldview and How Is It Used in Apologetics?

"Everyone has some kind of philosophy, some general worldview,
which to men of other views will seem mythological."

—H. RICHARD NIEBUHR, *Christ and Culture*

WHILE MANY HISTORIC APOLOGETIC arguments and methods provided valuable tools to defend the faith, they often merely confirmed the high probability of one aspect of belief rather than upholding the Christian faith as an entire system. For example, the various cosmological arguments demonstrated the need for a necessary First Cause, the forms of the teleological argument demonstrated a high probability of a Designer, and the moral arguments demonstrated the existence of a Moral Law Giver. At best, on their own, they led to a general form of theism rather than a singular, sound system that holds together and reflects reality. Other philosophies or religions may also produce solid arguments for certain aspects of their belief systems, so Christianity is not necessarily unique in this aspect. However, solitary arguments for individual beliefs do not demonstrate the truthfulness of the entire system, especially in comparison to other such systems of belief. No doubt, one may argue for some aspects of System A, while another may argue for aspects of System B, but that in itself does not demonstrate that System A as a whole is closer to the truth than System B (or any other systems that might exist). Only when one scrutinizes the system in its entirety for truthfulness can one honestly say that they have solid reasons for holding to the beliefs that they do.

Demonstrating the truthfulness of an entire system rather than merely arguing for individual aspects is where the concept of a belief structure being a worldview fits and why worldviews are the scope within which to perform the apologetic task. David Noebel explains that the battle for the hearts and minds of humanity happens at the level of worldview—the world's convictions about politics, ethics, science, and all other areas of contemporary thought come from a worldview. Therefore, having such a life commitment based on truth is of vital importance.[1] J. Mark Bertrand believes that the worldview concept has gained traction in scholarly debate and popular works for several reasons. First, the notion itself seems self-evident upon reflection. Second, it helps people realize in the ever-raging culture wars that people's perspectives on the other side of the cultural issues blind them from even considering opposing views—their beliefs being colored by "upbringing, class, ideology, and experience" (i.e., their worldview).[2] Thus, to take away such blindness, and to open eyes to the truths of reality, entails the testing of worldviews and defense of the one worldview that alone encapsulates truth (to a higher degree of probability than others).

However, to defend a worldview and its importance in the apologetic task, one must first understand what the idea of worldview entails. Defining worldview has not been an easy undertaking. Clement Vidal laments that "the term is unfortunately often used without any precise definition behind it."[3] A. Scott Moreau also notes, "Worldview is one of the most fascinating and frustrating terms used by evangelicals," and then aptly compares trying to define worldview as being like the attempt to nail ice cream to a wall.[4] Everyone has a worldview, a way in which they try to make sense of the world, and apologetics seeks to determine what worldview someone has and whether it is true.[5] The problem is that no single definition incor-

1. Noebel, *The Battle for Truth*, vii.
2. Bertrand, *Rethinking Worldview*, 21.
3. Vidal, "What Is a Worldview?" 1.
4. Moreau, "Hiebert's Legacy of Worldview," 223.
5. Brown, "Thinking Worldviewishly," 6.

porates what every scholar, philosopher, theologian, and apologist means when discussing this critical concept. Indeed, there are several similarities in definitions, but each definition has its own unique spin. Therefore, to make the statement that worldview is the scope or field within which the apologetic task occurs demands an understanding of where the concept originated and how it fits into the academic discussion, how scholars have defined the term, how this book will utilize the term, and how apologists have used the idea in their body of work. This overview and analysis will, in turn, justify the claim that apologetics done within the scope of testing the truthfulness of entire worldviews is an effective method.

The Birth and Growth of the Worldview Concept

Although worldviews, as they are, have always existed (in that everyone has a belief system about reality), reflection on the subject itself is somewhat recent in the history of philosophy, the sciences, and religion. Philosophy birthed the discussion of worldview and attempted to define the concept. Christian scholarship then borrowed the term and did much to flesh out its realization. Reflection on both its philosophical and religious foundations assists in demonstrating its usefulness in the apologetic task.

Philosophical Roots of Worldview as a Concept

Most scholars credit Immanuel Kant with being the first to coin the phrase "worldview" (German: *Weltanschauung*), where he utilized it to "accent the power of the perception of the human mind."[6] In his *Critique of Judgment*, Kant states,

> If the human mind is nonetheless to be able even to think the given infinite without contradiction, it must have within itself a power that is supersensible, whose idea of a noumenon cannot be intuited but can yet be regarded as the substrate underlying what is mere appearance, namely, our intuition of the world. For only by means of this power and its idea do we, in a pure intellectual estimation of magnitude, comprehend the infinite in the *world of sense* [Weltanschauung] entirely under a concept, even though in a mathematical estimation of magnitude by means of numerical concepts we can never think it in its entirety. Even a power

6. Naugle, *Worldview*, 58.

that enables us to think the infinite of supersensible intuition as given (in our intelligible substrate) surpasses any standard of sensibility.[7]

Within the context of his work, Kant spoke of one's sense of perception of the world. As Ted Cabal explains Kant's use of the term,

> The worldview concept came on the philosophical scene through Immanuel Kant's attempt to bolster science in response to Humean skepticism. It is appropriate that Kant coined the term *Weltanschauung*: in him the two mighty concourses of rationalism and empiricism converged and were bridged—and *Weltanschauung* with its optic and cognitive connotations provided a girder for the bridge. . . . In *Weltanschauung* Kant was seeking a comprehensive expression for the event of sight. The worldview is a sensory experience wherein the mind intuits the thing *underlying* the experience, the *Ding as sich*. It is an action whereby the phenomenon (the object as interpreted by the categories of the mind) signifies the noumenon (the inferred but unknowable source of experience). Kant, then, considered the worldview occasion to be more revelatory of the inherent structure of the human mind than of the world thus perceived. *Weltanschauung* in its very first use represented a subjectively conditioned experience.[8]

So, for Kant, a worldview is the view of the world from human sensory perception, from which human reason then arrives at an understanding of the world and where the individual fits within it.[9] Kant may have devised the term (although it never necessarily became an essential notion within his philosophy), but other philosophers expanded the concept from his initial usage.

The term gained momentum first in German philosophy, specifically in the thought-world of German Idealism and Romanticism.[10] Johann Gottlieb Fichte adopted the term for primarily the same use as Kant, as a form of "the perception of the sensible world." However, for him, it was more on the intuitive plane and less on the scientific.[11] Friedrich Wilhelm Joseph von Schelling embraced the term and changed the meaning so that it denoted

7. Kant, *Critique of* Judgment, 111–12. Emphasis mine.
8. Cabal, "The Worldview Concept," 1. Emphasis original.
9. Goheen and Bartholomew, *Living at the Crossroads*, 11–12.
10. Wolters, "Idea of Worldview," 15.
11. Naugle, *Worldview*, 60. Cabal, "The Worldview Concept," 1–2.

more of a way of apprehending and interpreting the universe.[12] Schelling's concept of worldview "touched on humanity's longing to come to terms with the deepest questions of existence and of the nature of the universe," and his handling of the worldview concept as a "comprehensive and cohesive understanding of the world" was highly influential for the philosophers who followed.[13] Georg Wilhelm Friedrich Hegel utilized worldview in seemingly various ways but generally spoke of it as a conceptual framework embedded in both the individual and national consciousness by which one forms a moral outlook on the world giving a practical perspective for moral obligation.[14] Scholars describe Hegel as having added a historical component to the concept, seeing worldview as "the total perception of nature, society and deity that changes according to the evolution of spirit," thus giving historical relativity to worldview, but it still has "'objectivity' for every epoch, nation and *Volksgeist*."[15]

Wilhelm Dilthey was one of the first to pioneer a systematic treatment of worldview.[16] Some even claim that history could rightly call him the father of the concept of worldview.[17] Michael Ermarth attests that "it was Dilthey who raised the problem of the world-views to a comprehensive theoretical statement. In this area he pioneered and mapped intellectual terrain which was later to be explored by students in many different disciplines. His writings provide full scale treatment of the genesis, articulation, comparison, and development of world-views."[18] For Dilthey, worldview was an intuition that grew to make sense of the riddle of life—through lived experience (such as expressed through art, religion, or metaphysics) as the mind attempts to make sense of existence.[19] From this, a worldview produces a philosophy, and the philosophy gives expression to the worldview.[20] However, this does not necessarily mean that worldviews are "consciously held or explicitly formulated"—they arise from intuition, striving to get

---

12. Naugle, *Worldview*, 60.

13. Goheen and Bartholomew, *Living at the Crossroads*, 12.

14. Naugle, *Worldview*, 69–70.

15. Becker, "Kierkegaard's Existential Philosophy," 1. Emphasis original.

16. Naugle, *Worldview*, 82.

17. Naugle, "Wilhelm Dilthey's Doctrine," 4.

18. Ermarth, *Wilhelm Dilthey*, 324.

19. Naugle, "Wilhelm Dilthey's Doctrine," 4–5. Naugle, *Worldview*, 83–84. Sire, *Naming the Elephant*, 27.

20. Wolters, "Idea of Worldview," 16.

beyond mere relativity to conceptual stability, although allowing the freedom to change and reformulate themselves when experience required it.[21]

Dilthey posited three features common to all worldviews: World picture (Weltbild), evaluation of life (Lebenswurdigung), and the ideals of the conduct of life (Lebensfuhrung). These three components "which correspond to the mental capacities of thinking, feeling, and willing, come together in a unified fashion under the dominance of any one of the three and form the structure of a world view."[22] Ermarth succinctly summarizes Dilthey's notion of a worldview when he writes,

> By virtue of the selective yet synthetic nature of consciousness, each individual gradually acquires a particular but comprehensive interpretation of his life in relation to the world, which Dilthey terms "world view." This world view is a combination of reflective, conscious awareness and pre-reflective interests and practical concerns. It relates one's own inner awareness of the world at large. The world view is a meaning-structure which gives coherence to the individual's ongoing experience. It is a synthesis of the basic and recurring "lived relations" and vital coherences which the person finds himself in. It provides consistency, integration, and stability in the face of the constant influx of new experiences. The world view, like the lived experience it synthesizes, is not simply the result of cognitive thinking, but of willing and feeling as well. All the capacities of mind are brought together in a functional coherence—though Dilthey came to hold that one capacity tends to predominate, giving direction to the others.[23]

Thus, worldviews for Dilthey are expressions of what is and what can be—conceptions of reality built from lived experiences. Worldviews would conflict as each expression of reality considered itself the only correct interpretation, but to avoid the clash of worldviews, one could "affirm their relativity without denying their validity."[24] Dilthey's own worldview shows through here—something can be both relative yet true regardless of the contradictions.

These early worldview philosophers offered differing views on whether a worldview was something unique to the individual or if it was something shared by a group or culture. For Kant, there was "one set of

---

21. Cabal, "The Worldview Concept," 4; Naugle, "Wilhelm Dilthey's Doctrine," 10.

22. Naugle, "Wilhelm Dilthey's Doctrine," 9.

23. Ermarth, *Wilhelm Dilthey*, 119.

24. Naugle, "Wilhelm Dilthey's Doctrine," 11.

determining categories for all rational minds, making a single basic view of the world possible."[25] However, for other philosophers, different people had different consciousness with various internal and external factors that shaped their worldview. Hegel saw worldview as a shared framework within a nation during a particular period that influences the individual; thus, the individuals living at a specific time in a specific society shared this worldview concurrently.[26] There were also noted differences between Kant and Dilthey. Michael Goheen and Craig Bartholomew observe, "Whereas Kant had believed that one worldview could be shared by all people (since all share in the human faculty of reason), Dilthey argued that (since, in his view, human understanding is profoundly conditioned by the individual's particular place and time in history) different worldviews are bound to arise from differing historical circumstances. He believed that all worldviews are but partial expressions of the universe and thus inevitably will clash with each other.[27]" It is not that Dilthey denied that individuals possessed worldviews, but he "primarily used the concept to denote the conceptions of reality that are shared and held communally during major historical epochs."[28] Dilthey also did not believe that worldviews dealt with mere abstractness. Whereas someone like Wilhelm Windelband "argues that all people implicitly appeal to universal values, thus implying that values have a metaphysical anchoring . . . or a supersensible reality in God," Dilthey instead "argued that thought is historically relative and is grounded in evolutionary naturalism."[29]

Entering the twentieth century, not all philosophers saw worldview as a positive concept. Edmund Husserl considered worldview philosophy, along with naturalism and historicism, as a threat to philosophy proper (the foundation of all sciences) due to what he viewed as its lethal epistemic relativism.[30] Still, in railing against worldview philosophy, Husserl granted the academic world his own characterization of the worldview concept. For Husserl, worldview philosophy "gives in the great systems the relatively most perfect answer to the riddles of life and the world, namely that achieves in the best way possible the solution and satisfactory

25. Naugle, *Worldview*, 69.

26. Naugle, *Worldview*, 71.

27. Goheen and Bartholomew, *Living at the Crossroads*, 13.

28. Naugle, "Wilhelm Dilthey's Doctrine," 11.

29. Cabal, "The Worldview Concept," 3.

30. Naugle, *Worldview*, 110.

clarification of the theoretical, axiological, practical inconsistencies of life, that experience, wisdom, and mere world- and life-view are able to overcome only incompletely."[31] Husserl did not see worldview as something an individual developed and held. He states, "Worldview in this determinate sense, though one that includes a variety of types and valuational gradations, is—and this need not be further elaborated—no mere achievement of an isolated personality, which would be an abstraction anyway; the personality belongs to a cultural community and an age, and it makes good sense in relation to its most pronounced forms to speak of the culture and worldview not only of a particular individual but also of the age."[32] For Husserl, worldview needed to step aside to make way for the rigorous science of true philosophy.

Karl Jaspers perceived worldview as a mental frame of reference with a subjective side (attitudes) emanating from mental patterns formed in experiencing existence and an objective side (world pictures), which is the developed world of objects.[33] It is a "natural (not explicitly chosen) attitude realized in life-experience and typical for a certain reference-set (a time, place, nation, subgroup)."[34] A person forms a mental picture as their attitudes encounter the world, constituting a worldview.[35] Some see this as a nearly postmodern take on the concept of worldview since Jaspers did not seek absolute objective knowledge, nor did he ask "questions about the objective or metaphysical correctness of worldview contents because worldviews have their foundation in 'the reality of the mind.'"[36] Thus, for Jaspers, worldviews were human psychological formations with no necessary correlation to external reality.

Martin Heidegger strongly contrasted what he saw to be the relativism of the concept of worldview with the more rigorous scientific undertaking of philosophy.[37] In contrasting his conception of philosophy with the ideas of worldview that permeated philosophical thought at the time, Heidegger conceived worldview not just as theoretical knowledge but as conceptions

31. Husserl, "Philosophy as Rigorous Science," 285.

32. Husserl, "Philosophy as Rigorous Science," 285.

33. Naugle, *Worldview*, 121.

34. Goldman, "Psychology of Worldviews," 32.

35. Naugle, *Worldview*, 121.

36. Cabal, "The Worldview Concept," 5.

37. Naugle, *Worldview*, 128.

and interpretations of natural things born from human experience.[38] Still, he opposed worldview both as a method and content since he believed these limited views inhibit an encounter with being: "He seeks a recovery of being, but the depiction of the world in objectivist terms as a picture blocks this perception."[39] Worldview seemed to get in the way of Heidegger's purpose of philosophy.

Ludwig Wittgenstein rejected worldview as a residual of Cartesian foundationalism, "for each and every one of them pretends to what is impossible—an intellectual grasp of reality as it really is."[40] Instead, he offered a world picture (Weltbild) akin to worldview as previously conceived. World pictures form one's conception of the world and its character as inherited by one's life-context. They give a narrative that functions as a governing mythology promulgated rhetorically and accepted by faith.[41] As Sire indicates, world picture and worldview are seemingly synonymous. If one were to give voice to Wittgenstein's cryptic and obscure ideas, it would read, "A worldview is a way of thinking about reality that rejects the notion that one can have 'knowledge' of objective reality (that is, know any 'truth' about any nonlinguistic reality) and thus limits knowable reality to the language one finds useful in getting what one wants."[42]

Although the philosophers discussed above are by no means the sole forerunners of the philosophical birth and growth of the concept of worldview, they are representative of the critical times and thoughts of its development. Philosophy gave birth to the recognition of worldview and gave its scholarly usage much of its form, yet one could say it outgrew its original intention. Although connected, it is right to consider worldview as different from philosophy. Philosophies themselves are worldviews, so one could say that worldviews give explanation and expression to a philosophy. However, worldviews give expression to much more than philosophical systems, but also other forms of systematic thought. Tawa Anderson, W. Michael Clark, and David Naugle recognize that other German thinkers such as Ranke (history), Wagner (music), and von Humboldt (physics) applied the worldview concept to their disciplines as well.[43] Not long after, Christian theol-

---

38. Naugle, *Worldview*, 136–37.

39. Naugle, *Worldview*, 144.

40. Sire, *Naming the Elephant*, 29.

41. Naugle, *Worldview*, 158–61

42. Sire, *Naming the Elephant*, 30.

43. Anderson, Clark, and Naugle, *Introduction to Christian Worldview*, 9.

ogy adopted and embraced the idea of worldview and used it for its unique purposes, expanding its definition and reach. This, in a sense, opened the door and blazed the trail for its use in apologetics.

The Christian Expansion of the Worldview Concept

Christian thinkers and academics were some of the first to appropriate the concept of worldview and expand its use within their system of thought. Although based on what had come before within philosophic thinking, Christian scholars and theologians brought their own nuance to the concept, which would then compare systems of thought for truthfulness. Although this work expands on the apologetic value, it is imperative to consider the Christian use and definition of the worldview concept to understand how worldview is the scope within which truth-testing can transpire.

One might consider Søren Kierkegaard as a forefather to the Christian procurement of worldview thinking. Like previous philosophers, he noted a difference between philosophy and worldview, "arguing that whereas philosophy is an objective system of thought (held, as it were, at arm's length), worldview is a set of beliefs held so closely by an individual that it is appropriate to speak of living within or owning one's worldview."[44] Kierkegaard coined a closely related term: life-view. For Kierkegaard,

> A life-view . . . is more than an aggregate, a sum-total of propositions affirmed in their abstract impartiality; it is more than experience, which as such is always atomistic, for it (a life-view) is the transubstantiation of experience, it is hard-won certainty in itself, unshakable by any experience, whether it has merely oriented itself in all the circumstances of the world (a merely human standpoint, Stoicism, for example), which thereby holds back from being touched by any deeper experience—or whether in its direction toward heaven (the religious) it has found in that the central focus, both for its heavenly and earthly existence, has gained the true Christian assurance.[45]

Life-view played a crucial role in his existential thought. As Vincent Mc-Carthy explains,

> Life-view emphasizes the duty and importance of the individual to understand himself both his "premises" and his "conclusions," his

44. Goheen and Bartholomew, *Living at the Crossroads*, 12.
45. Kierkegaard, "Af En Endu Levendes Papirer," 6–8.

conditionality and his freedom. Each man must answer for himself about the meaning of life, and thus he cannot take his cue from the spirit of the age which will all too readily answer on his behalf. In addition, life-view, as philosophy of life, challenges established, academic philosophy which proceeds exclusively from thought. The new philosophy which Kierkegaard suggests by his emphasis on life-view and his definition of it is no longer detached thought but reflection upon the meaning of experience and then its articulation in a coherent view. Life-view is not to be the sole aspect of new philosophizing, but will instead properly take its place at the center of the search for wisdom, which philosophy once claimed to be.[46]

Although seemingly synonymous, some see the distinction as important. For example, Hjördis Becker thinks the distinctiveness of life-view is that it "translates the *epistemological* concept of German Idealism into an *existential* concept with *ethical* dimensions."[47]

Scholarship has chiefly credited James Orr and Abraham Kuyper with appropriating worldview thought for Christian consideration, reaching "for the concept of worldview in response to the post-Enlightenment culture that was coming to dominate the West."[48] Although Orr and Kuyper are generally given credit for the Christian embrace of the worldview concept, some, such as Eilert Herms, would disagree, believing instead that the trend first emerged among liberal theologians, stating, "In the history of the problem of worldview within Protestant theology, the positions of Schleiermacher and Ritschl actually constitute the base point and a turning point. Schleiermacher was the very first theology [*sic*] who used the concept of worldview in a theoretically concise setting. And Ritschl then elevated the concept to a central instrument of theological theory construction."[49] This, however, goes against most scholarly works on the subject.

As James Orr defines his conception of the term,

The word "Weltanschauung," [is] sometimes interchanged with another compound of the same signification, "Weltansicht." Both words mean literally "view of the world," but whereas the phrase in English is limited by associations which connect it predominatingly with physical nature, in German the word is not thus limited, but has almost the force of a technical term, denoting the widest

46. McCarthy, *The Phenomenology of Moods*, 136–37.
47. Becker, "From Weltanschauung to Livs-Anskuelse," 2. Emphasis original.
48. Goheen and Bartholomew, *Living at the Crossroads*, 14.
49. Herms, "'Weltanschaunng' Bei Friedrich Schleiermacher," 123.

view which the mind can take of things in the effort to grasp them together as a whole from the standpoint of some particular philosophy or theology. To speak, therefore, of a "Christian view of the world" implies that Christianity also has its highest point of view, and its view of life connected therewith, and that this, when developed, constitutes an ordered whole.[50]

As Oliphint further explains,

Orr's interest in world view was a result of his expertise in German theology and philosophy. The more he read of the German literature, the more he encountered the word *Weltanschauung* and related concepts. What struck him, as a pastor and apologist, was just how neatly Christianity fit into the concerns of those who were attempting to develop a conceptual worldview. Because Christianity, as truth, is a coherent system of truth, it (and Orr will argue, it alone) can address the concerns that are a part of world view thinking. Orr was convinced that nothing less than the comprehensive truth of Christianity could answer the attacks and critiques that were prevalent in his day.[51]

Although Orr recognized that the use of the term and concept of worldview had just become common in the prior two or three decades of his writing this work, he also recognized that worldview is as old as thought itself, writing,

The thing itself [i.e., worldview] is as old as the dawn of reflection, and is found in a cruder or more advanced form in every religion and philosophy with any pretensions to a historical character. The simplest form in which we meet with it is in the rude, tentative efforts at a general explanation of things in the cosmogonies and theogonies of most ancient religions, the mythological character of which need not blind us to the rational motive which operates in them. With the growth of philosophy, a new type of world-view is developed—that which attempts to explain the universe as a system by the help of some general principle or principles (water, air, number, etc.), accompanied by the use of terms which imply the conception of an All or Whole of things.[52]

Orr went on to explain that he saw two causes that lead to the formation of worldviews. The first is speculative or theoretical in that the mind attempts

50. Orr, *Christian View of God*, 3.

51. Oliphint, "The Reformed World View," 6. Emphasis original.

52. Orr, *Christian View of God*, 5.

to bring unity to the fragmented facts and information with which it interacts, endeavoring to form a general law or positive theory that answers the great questions of life. The second cause is a practical motive wherein someone desires to determine their place in the world and by what principles they ought to conduct themselves.[53] Then if someone is to hold onto a worldview, it must cohere with the universe, for the universe is one and has one set of laws that holds it together. So, if one embraces Christianity, although not a scientific system, one can reconcile it with evident and established results in science. Although not a philosophy per se, its conclusions are in harmony with sound reason. Christianity, along with other worldviews, gives account for and gives interpretations to the facts, binding them together to give voice to an ultimate principle.[54]

Theologian and statesman Abraham Kuyper was familiar with the concept of worldview early in his career. Yet, any hint of the idea in his work was "loose and undefined, and occurred in a way that was more incidental than purposeful."[55] Peter Heslam notes three elements in Kuyper's early thoughts that contributed to his embrace of the worldview concept: the need for unity and coherency in thought, the need for a single principle, and the need for an alternative system to Paganism and Modernism.[56] It was not until the Stone Lectures at Princeton Seminary that Kuyper would fully incorporate worldview into his body of work.[57] After having interacted with Orr's work, Kuyper used the lectures to establish Calvinism as a complete belief system that related to the whole of life. Calling it the synonymous "life system," Kuyper saw the times within which he lived as a struggle between competing systems of thought—especially modernism against Calvinism.[58] Kuyper did not spend much time defining what he meant by life system other than implying that it is an insight into the universe that deals with three fundamental relations of all human life: man's relation to God, man's relation to man, and man's relation to the world.[59] And yet Kuyper led the way for the concept to be the scope of a Christian's interaction with the world, both in practical and scholarly areas. Richard

53. Orr, *Christian View of God*, 6–7.

54. Orr, *Christian View of God*, 8–9.

55. Heslam, *Creating a Christian Worldview*, 90.

56. Heslam, *Creating a Christian Worldview*, 92.

57. Edgar and Oliphint, *Christian Apologetics Past and Present*, 2:334.

58. Kuyper, *Calvinism*, 3–4.

59. Kuyper, *Calvinism*, 16.

Mouw notes, "This focus on worldview has been our way of following Kuyper's lead in insisting that our cultural involvements, including our scholarly pursuits, have to be consciously guided by our understanding of our place in the larger scheme of things."[60]

Kuyper takes note that he borrowed life-system/worldview concepts from Orr, mentioning that Orr observes that

> the German technical term *Weltanschauung* has no precise equivalent in English. [Orr] therefore used the literal translation *view of the world*, notwithstanding this phrase in English is limited by associations, which connect it predominatingly with *physical* nature. For this reason . . . one explicit phrase: *life and world view* seems to be preferable. My American friends however told me that the shorter phrase: *life system*, on the other side of the ocean, is often used in the same sense. So lecturing before an American public . . . I interchanged alternately both phrases, of *life-system* and *life and world view* in accordance with the special meaning predominating in my argumentation.[61]

For Kuyper, from the standpoint of particular worldviews, it was Calvinism that was "an all-embracing life-system, rather than a narrowly defined set of doctrines or a particular ecclesiology."[62] Calvinism was an alternative life system that was as equally valid as any other (sharing in many of the same fundamental characteristics as other life-systems) and was functional as a culture-shaping force. As Albert Wolters further explains, for Kuyper, Calvinism was "a complete worldview with implications for all of life, implications which must be worked out and applied in such areas as politics, art, and scholarship."[63] However, whatever terminology one might use and whether one held to Calvinistic views of Christianity or not, "Kuyper maintained that Christians must have a comprehensive view of all of life from a Scriptural perspective, which is the basis for their choices and informs all their actions. It deals with the most fundamental issues of life: *Where did we come from? Why are we here? Where are we going? How do we get there?* . . . A biblical worldview is necessarily antithetical to all competing views in every domain of life."[64]

---

60. Mouw, *Abraham Kuyper*, 90.

61. Kuyper, *Calvinism*, 3n1. Emphasis original.

62. Heslam, *Creating a Christian Worldview*, 88.

63. Wolters, "On the Idea of Worldview," 20.

64. McGoldrick, "Claiming Every Inch," 32.

James D. Bratt notes that Kuyper readily welcomed the worldview concept into his arsenal for several reasons. First, worldview was a recognition that both groups and individuals "operated out of a cognitive framework that was itself not established by reason or science." Second, the concept of worldview promised "coherence in a rapidly expanding universe of knowledge, rendering an ordered whole out of what otherwise would remain a jumble of data." Third, since worldviews embrace the whole world, it "thus established a mandate for critical Christian comprehensiveness." Finally, the concept of worldview was highly democratic in that "it assumed a pluralistic situation, was designed for popular reception, and sought to inspire action."[65] In his lectures, then, Kuyper argues that worldview affects how humans interact with the gambit of human endeavors, including the crucial subjects of religion, politics, science, and art. In his theological work on art, David A. Covington rightly notes (in what one could consider a very worldview-ish statement) that "a person does not live in a sequence of separate compartments," but he later wrote that "Abraham Kuyper invokes Calvin in arguing for art as an independent cultural category, free of everything, even of Christian doctrine."[66] That statement, however, would appear to go against Kuyper's whole point that the Calvinistic worldview speaks into every aspect of a Christian's life—not living in separate compartments.

Kuyper's thought had a significant influence on fellow Dutchman Herman Dooyeweerd. In his early works, Dooyeweerd agreed that worldviews undergird one's life and thought. Later in life, he argued that spiritual and religious factors played a more significant role in shaping someone's beliefs and interpretations of the world than did the abstract concept of worldview.[67] For Dooyeweerd, religion is the deepest part of the heart from which someone interprets reality, while philosophy and worldview are more cognitive. Although philosophy and worldview have some commonalities, worldview is one's engagement in life, while philosophy is theoretical and detached from life.[68] Dooyeweerd gives an extensive explanation of the difference between worldview and philosophy, writing,

> The concept "life- and world-view" is raised above the level of vague representations burdened either with resentment or with exaggerated veneration only if it is understood in the sense that

65. Bratt, *Abraham Kuyper*, 207–8.

66. Covington, *Redemptive Theology of Art*, 41, 102.

67. Naugle, *Worldview*, 25–26.

68. Naugle, *Worldview*, 29.

is necessarily inherent in it *as a view of* totality. . . . It is not, as such, of a theoretical character. Its view of totality is not the *theoretical,* but rather the *pretheoretical.* It does not conceive reality in its abstracted modal aspects of meaning, but rather in typical structures of individuality which are not analyzed in a theoretical way. It is not restricted to a special category of "philosophic thinkers," but applies to everybody, the simplest included. . . . Therefore philosophy and a life- and world-view are *in the root* absolutely united with each other, even though they may not be identified. Philosophy cannot take the place of a life- and world-view, nor the reverse, for the *task* of each of the two is different. They must rather understand each other mutually from their common religious root. Yet, to be sure, philosophy has to give a theoretical account of a life- and world-view.[69]

Although different, the two concepts work together in that philosophy can theoretically analyze worldview and its values, describing and clarifying what a worldview tries to convey.[70] Still, it is a worldview that gives direction to one's existence as it gives voice to that which rises within the heart and unifies that which is disjointed in thought and life.

By the end of the twentieth century, the use of worldview within Christian scholarship had strong roots and became a norm in dealing with various areas of academia (be it theology, apologetics, or missions). Therefore, scholarship turned toward analyzing the idea of worldview itself. Several scholars examined the concept and gave form to what religion and philosophy meant by the term "worldview." Since the term or its equivalents came into such common usage, it was necessary to define through words what such an abstract concept entailed.

Arthur Holmes observes that to find the distinctiveness of thought and characteristics, one must study both the unifying perspectives of an entire tradition and the variables shaping particular formulations of a worldview. Worldviews begin at the pre-philosophical level, "without either systematic planning or theoretical intentions with the beliefs and attitudes and values on which people act."[71] There are unanalyzed, underlying beliefs that, upon reflection, shape and develop the view one takes. This pre-philosophical level "unifies and guides thought and action and defines the highest good"

---

69. Dooyeweerd, *Critique of Theoretical Thought,* 127–28. Emphasis original.

70. Dooyeweerd, *Critique of Theoretical Thought,* 133.

71. Holmes, *Contours of a World View,* 31–32.

into a singular unifying perspective.[72] A worldview entails how this unifying perspective guides and interprets different areas of reality, be it theology, philosophy, science, economic, political, or social, among others. Holmes emphasizes that just because a worldview embodies beliefs and values (and sometimes stories) does not mean it is purely subjective (such as in pluralism and relativism). The charge of subjectivism is false since one may objectively demonstrate (through proofs, evidence, and arguments) the truthfulness of many beliefs and values. Therefore, worldviews themselves are demonstrable as true or false (although this does not deny that there is much in a worldview that is pre-philosophical and thereby beyond proof).[73]

Ronald Nash describes a worldview as a "conceptual scheme by which we consciously or unconsciously place or fit everything we believe and by which we interpret and judge reality."[74] A worldview contains the answers a person has for the primary questions in life and is the pattern by which they arrange their beliefs.[75] Nash believes that a well-rounded worldview holds beliefs in five significant areas: God, metaphysics, epistemology, ethics, and anthropology.[76] He notes that just because a group of people adheres to the same worldview does not mean that they will agree on the interpretation and judgment of every single issue of life. Where there is a disagreement between two adherents to a worldview, it behooves them to demonstrate how their view is more consistent with the basic tenets of their worldview than any other view.[77] He also emphasizes the importance of presuppositions—assumed beliefs that one holds without the support of arguments or evidence. He likens them to train tracks that have no switches—they determine the direction and destination of the person who holds them.[78]

David Naugle, who provides the seminal work on the worldview concept philosophically and religiously, rightfully notes that a theory or definition of worldview itself is a function of the worldview of the one doing the defining.[79] There is no neutral ground from which to work with the idea. However, upon reflection on how the concept itself has developed over

---

72. Holmes, *Contours of a World View*, 33.

73. Holmes, *Contours of a World View*, 45–49.

74. Nash, *Worldviews in Conflict*, 16.

75. Nash, *Life's Ultimate Questions*, 13.

76. Nash, *Worldviews in Conflict*, 26; Nash, *Life's Ultimate Questions*, 14–17.

77. Nash, *Life's Ultimate Questions*, 17.

78. Nash, *Life's Ultimate Questions*, 20; Nash, *Worldviews in Conflict*, 21–23.

79. Naugle, *Worldview*, 253.

time, Naugle defines worldview as "a semiotic system of narrative signs that creates the definitive symbolic universe which is responsible in the main for the shape of a variety of life-determining, human practices. It creates the channels in which the waters of reason flow. It establishes the horizons of an interpreter's point of view by which texts of all types are understood. It is that mental medium by which the world is known. The human heart is its home, and it provides a home for the human heart."[80] For Naugle, worldviews are systems of signs and symbols (be they words or otherwise) occupying the human heart that set the course for belief and practice. The answers to the essential questions of life that these signs represent are not only expressed in a proposition but also through narrative. As he intimates, stories have the power to establish a context for life.[81] Worldview is a semiotic conceptualization of reality, giving shape and content to human consciousness, through which one interprets the nature of things, answering the most profound questions of life and existence, that one might grasp some semblance of understanding of the human condition.[82]

James Sire also produced a formative work regarding worldview. He first intuits that worldviews have a pre-theoretical or presuppositional dimension that underlies and influences theoretical thought and practical action.[83] Other scholars would further develop this seminal idea of worldview. For example, Craig Bartholomew further elaborates by explaining that "a worldview is distinct from philosophy, because a worldview is *pretheoretical*. By pretheoretical we mean that it is not a logical, systematic theory, as is found in traditional philosophy. Beliefs are distinct from opinions or feelings because they make a cognitive claim. They are also committed in the sense that they are not just opinions or hypotheses. The beliefs constituting a worldview are also basic because they deal with matters of ultimate significance, such as what life is all about, what happens at death, the problem of evil, and so on and so forth."[84] Anderson, Clark, and Naugle also concur, stating, "Worldviews are pretheoretical in nature; they develop prior to or devoid of conscious reflection and rational deliberation."[85] Albert Wolters calls the worldview concept "prescientific," stating, "A worldview is a

---

80. Naugle, *Worldview*, 329–30.

81. Naugle, *Worldview*, 297.

82. Naugle, *Worldview*, 345.

83. Sire, *Naming the Elephant*, 109.

84. Bartholomew, *Contours of the Kuyperian Tradition*, 126. Emphasis original.

85. Anderson, Clark, and Naugle, *Introduction to Christian Worldview*, 14.

matter of the shared everyday experience of humankind, an inescapable component of all human knowing, and as such it is nonscientific, or rather (since scientific knowing is always dependent on the intuitive knowing of our everyday experience) *prescientific,* in nature. It belongs to an order of cognition more basic than that of science or theory."[86]

Sire notes that worldviews are assumptions a person holds consciously or unconsciously; neither a worldview nor any aspect of it need be at the conscious level. A worldview need not answer every possible question about life that someone may raise—a person may not grasp that they have a worldview or be able to articulate it, yet whatever is relevant to a person's life situation is lived out from their worldview.[87] He makes the critical note that worldviews do not remain an intellectual category, nor are they merely an interpretation of the universe. Instead, they are more of an orientation of the soul or spirit and inextricably tied to lived experience and behavior, guiding one's decisions.[88] As Schultz and Swezey comment, "Sire's main point is that worldview is not strictly about information, beliefs, or knowledge, but must entail 'heart-orientation' and behavior as well," then explain that by heart they mean the religious, intellectual, affective, and volitional center of a person.[89] A. Steven Evans agrees as he writes that "life transformation takes place at the heart level. To change the heart is to change worldview. To change worldview is to change culture."[90] Thus heart, as well as mind, is essential in worldview considerations. Sire further notes that narratives and stories often transmit a worldview. These stories come together to tell one master story—a metanarrative by which people interpret the world around them.[91] His analysis leads to an all-inclusive definition: "A worldview is a commitment, a fundamental orientation of the heart, that can be expressed as a story or in a set of presuppositions (assumptions which may be true, partially true or entirely false) which we hold (consciously or subconsciously, consistently or inconsistently) about the basic constitution of reality, and that provides the foundation on which we live and move and have our being."[92]

---

86. Wolters, *Creation Regained*, 10. Emphasis original.
87. Sire, *Naming the Elephant*, 112.
88. Sire, *Naming the Elephant*, 117.
89. Schultz and Swezey, "Three-Dimensional Concept of Worldview," 231, 237.
90. Evans, "Matters of the Heart," 186.
91. Sire, *Naming the Elephant*, 119–20.
92. Sire, *Naming the Elephant*, 141.

Missiological anthropologist Paul Hiebert looks at worldview from the dimension of the community, defining it as the "fundamental cognitive, affective, and evaluative presuppositions a group of people make about the nature of things, and which they use to order their lives;" it is what "people in a community take as given realities, the maps they have of reality that they use for living."[93] He distinguishes two dimensions: a cognitive dimension that organizes one's assumptions and ideas about the nature of the universe, and an affective dimension where one experiences, exhibits, values, and acts on emotions.[94] From this foundation, Hiebert identifies six worldview functions: (1) worldviews are the plausibility structures that provide answers to life's ultimate questions, (2) worldviews provide emotional security, (3) worldviews validate cultural norms used to evaluate experiences and choose courses of action, (4) worldviews help integrate culture, (5) worldviews monitor culture change, and (6) worldviews provide psychological reassurance that the world indeed is as the person sees it.[95]

Several other scholars help sharpen our understanding of the worldview concept. Norm Geisler and Willian Watkins reveal that a worldview attempts to explain all of reality—all the relationships between things and events in the whole of existence—rather than just one or a few aspects of it.[96] Worldview integrates all the parts into a meaningful whole. William Brown writes that a worldview entails three crucial elements: an explanation of the world, an interpretation of the world, and an application of this view toward life.[97] This practical/applicational aspect of worldview is quite important, for as Kenneth Samples explains, "worldviews shape, influence and generally direct a person's life, because people behave as they believe, their worldviews guide their thoughts, attitudes, values, interpretations, perspectives, decisions, and actions."[98] Lars Haikola emphasizes that a worldview is not only a way to understand the world and a pattern for interpretations but also a pattern for action.[99] J. Mark Bertrand observes that, in some sense, people choose their worldview, where one's choices shape subsequent approaches to interpretation. Yet, in another sense, a

---

93. Hiebert, *Transforming Worldviews*, loc. 271–73, Kindle.

94. Story, *Christianity on the Offense*, 227.

95. Hiebert, *Transforming Worldviews*, loc. 541–65, Kindle.

96. Geisler and Watkins, *Worlds Apart*, 11.

97. Brown, "Thinking Worldviewishly," 6.

98. Samples, *A World of Difference*, 21.

99. Haikola, "Need for a World-View," 767.

worldview chooses a person, where life circumstances form the range within which someone operates.[100] Mark L. Ward suggests that worldviews include three elements: first, a worldview contains a head-heart system of fundamental beliefs, assumptions, and values; second, a worldview tells a big story about the world; and third, a worldview produces action.[101] Graham Cole distinguishes two ways of looking at the worldview concept: the existential worldview focuses on real questions about existence, while the encyclopedic worldview attempts to give an account of all that comes before the human consciousness.[102] Arlie J. Hoover notes that all worldviews transcend empirical reality; therefore, all worldviews entail some form of faith—still based on evidence, but not perfect evidence.[103]

As with philosophy, there is some debate within Christian scholarship over whether worldview is unique to the individual, the collective, or both. Brian J. Walsh and J. Richard Middleton observe that while the individual holds a worldview, they are never alone in having a worldview. Worldviews are shared and communal and are the roots of a culture that orients a people in certain beliefs.[104] W. T. Jones notes that worldviews have both an individual and a group or societal dimension. He writes that it is possible to talk about the worldview of a group, "providing that modes of the individual members of that group or society tend to ground around some mode. The central tendencies of the individual members of the group in question will doubtless differ widely, but they nonetheless fall into a distribution that is characteristic of this society during this time-period and that differs from the distribution for this society during some other time-period or for other societies."[105] His definition of worldview is unique, comprehensive, and helpful to the overall discussion, as he writes, "The world view of any individual is a set of very wide-range vectors in that individual's belief space (a) that he learned early in life and that are not readily changed and (b) that have a determinate influence on much of his observable behavior, both verbal and nonverbal, but (c) that he seldom or never verbalizes in the referential mode, though (d) they are constantly conveyed by him in

---

100. Bertrand, *Rethinking Worldview*, 29–30.

101. Ward, et al., *Biblical Worldview*, 6–15.

102. Cole, *Do Christians Have a Worldview?*, 4.

103. Hoover, *Dear Agnos*, 15–16.

104. Walsh and Middleton, *The Transforming Vision*, 31–33.

105. Jones, "World Views," 86.

the expressive mode and as latent meanings."[106] N. T. Wright contends that worldviews "form the grid through which humans, both individually and in social groupings, perceive all of reality."[107] Although individuals hold a grid for perceiving reality unto themselves, a shared worldview is found where groups of individuals have grids containing numerous points of agreement.

While worldviews can reflect the culture where adherents express them, and culture can be a reflection of the prevailing worldview, I am hesitant to equate a shared worldview solely with culture since some people in the same culture may hold very diverse worldviews (even with certain points of commonalities).[108] One American of European ancestry may be a Christian, while their neighbor of a similar heritage is an atheist, yet they both culturally hold to the same American ideals (be it the notion of freedom or otherwise). They may share a culture but do not share a worldview since their answers to some of life's most significant questions diverge entirely. While a person has one worldview—one belief structure—Harold Netland indicates that someone can participate in several cultures. Netland gives an example: "A Pakistani Muslim immigrant to the United States might at the same time be part of American culture, second-generation Pakistani immigrant culture, Islamic culture, and the culture of doctoral students at the University of Chicago. Each of these cultural contexts is somewhat distinctive, but there is no difficulty in saying that the same person participates in each of them."[109] Then again, people from different cultures may share a worldview, as is the case of an American Christian and an African Christian—their cultures are entirely different, but the way they view the world and answer life's significant questions may be the same. There are worldview aspects to culture, and I believe that a worldview can shape a culture, and diverse worldviews may hold characteristics that make sharing a culture possible, but they are not equal. A group holds a worldview when the individuals share beliefs regarding life's ultimate questions. A group shares a culture when the individuals are a part of a society in which they have a shared distribution of knowledge, ideas, concepts, and symbols.[110] Harold Netland notes that one can speak of a worldview as being true or normative for all people throughout all time; one cannot say

106. Jones, "World Views," 83
107. Wright, *The New Testament*, 32.
108. Hiebert, *Transforming Worldviews*, loc. 276, Kindle.
109. Netland, *Christianity & Religious Diversity*, 37.
110. Carley, "Theory of Group Stability," 333.

the same for culture.[111] Although worldview and culture obviously overlap, they are not synonymous.

Another interesting aspect of worldview found in more recent scholarship is that a worldview tells a story, and one can articulate a worldview through that story. Goheen and Bartholomew bring this aspect to the fore when they define worldview as "an articulation of the basic beliefs embedded in a shared grand story that are rooted in a faith commitment and that give shape and direction to the whole of our individual and corporate lives."[112] Anderson, Clark, and Naugle explain that "the philosophical and religious beliefs of human beings are more commonly shared and passed down through story, not through a set of philosophical propositions. We are storied creatures, responding more readily to narrative than to doctrine."[113] N. T. Wright notes that story-telling humans find themselves in a story-laden world and create a story through their observations. When a challenge bears upon someone's story (that is, that the story's claims about reality might be mistaken), one can find through further narrative alternative ways of speaking honestly about the world using new or modified stories. "What this means is that one must constantly subject data to testing and verification so he can spiral-in on the truth."[114] Oral and written literature as stories serve to reinforce worldview assumptions in seven ways. Evans argues,

1. It provides a basis of common origins and identity;

2. It answers questions about human destiny and what may help or alter it;

3. It reinforces basic assumptions of authority, respect, and rights to land or other material possessions;

4. It clearly pictures who are to be included and who are to be excluded, who are the "we" and who are the "they;"

5. It teaches and reinforces moral values;

6. It serves to illustrate ideal and sub-ideal behavior and the rewards and punishments that go along with either;

7. It serves as encouragement in times of difficulty and uncertainty.[115]

---

111. Netland, *Christianity & Religious Diversity*, 38.

112. Goheen and Bartholomew, *Living at the Crossroads*, 23.

113. Anderson, Clark, and Naugle, *Introduction to Christian Worldview*, 14.

114. Fesko, "Wright on Prolegomena," 10.

115. Evans, "Matters of the Heart," 189–90.

However, story and narrative not only form a worldview, they can also transform—bringing change to the individual life and the group.[116] Bertrand suggests that stories can both develop a personal history for the individual and create a way for communities to view themselves collectively.[117] Jill Carattini asserts,

> The world of belief-systems and worldviews is indeed a complicated playground of stories, storytellers, passions, and allegiances. . . . What makes the interplay of story most complicated is our inability often to name or even perceive these interacting powers in the first place. That which permeates our surroundings, subconsciously molds our understanding, and continuously informs our vision of reality is not always easy to articulate. . . . These deeply rooted ideologies are challenged only when a different ideology or imagination comes knocking, when a different faith-system comes along and upsets the imagination that powerfully orders our world. . . . Whether Christian, atheist, or Hindu, no one can avoid being in the world. We cannot escape the world's formative stories.[118]

Conceiving worldviews as stories does not negate their truthfulness, for stories are the vessel through which one articulates the truth of a worldview. Smaller stories and narratives flesh out the overall story—the metanarrative that embodies a worldview.

Final Summary of Worldview

Having thus walked through the history of the development and definition of the concept leaves the groundwork for defining worldview for the field of apologetics. I consider worldview to be a systematized belief structure and heart orientation held by individuals and shared by groups beginning at a presuppositional level which, consciously or unconsciously, leads to a particular interpretation of reality. Although one may not be able to articulate every facet of their beliefs completely, a worldview influences a person's attitudes, choices, and behaviors in their interaction with the world in all its aspects. The one who holds this systematic belief structure and heart orientation may not be capable of demonstrating or proving the truth or falsity of this system and still have some epistemic warrant for believing

116. Evans, "Matters of the Heart," 190.
117. Bertrand, *Rethinking Worldview*, 101.
118. Carattini, "The Unstoppable Story."

it. However, one may still hold the system itself up to scrutiny; that is, one can test the claims that one's worldview makes about reality. Therefore, an inquirer can prove or disprove the system as a whole. The holder of the systematic belief structure does not always articulate their worldview through direct, propositional statements but at times uses stories and narratives to convey held beliefs; nevertheless, the truths expressed in any of these forms, and the grand metanarrative to which they point, are testable for truthfulness or falseness.

Worldview Apologetics

Since the scholarly inquiry and use of worldview is a somewhat recent development, the defense of Christianity as a worldview and the scrutinization of other philosophies and religions as worldviews is also recent. There has been a slow development of worldview apologetics, beginning with James Orr and then down through apologists such as Francis Schaeffer, laying the groundwork for the approach discussed in this work that several apologists now use. So, understanding apologetics from the scope of worldview requires understanding what has developed to this point.

James Orr

James Orr, who introduced worldview to the Christian sphere, recognized that worldview was the domain from which apologetics ought to take place. Since the attacks of modernity in his day were not piecemeal but comprehensive, the work of apologetics ought to be in maintaining truthfulness or falseness at the level of systematized belief structures—the scope of worldview. Orr writes,

> I have deliberately chosen [the subject of worldview] for this very reason, that it enables me to deal with Christianity in its entirety or as a system, instead of dealing with particular aspects or doctrines of it. Both methods have their advantages; but no one, I think, whose eyes are open to the signs of the times, can fail to perceive that if Christianity is to be effectually defended from the attacks made upon it, it is the comprehensive method which is rapidly becoming the more urgent. . . . It is the Christian view of things in general which is attacked, and it is by an exposition and

vindication of the Christian view of things as a whole that the attack can most successfully be met.[119]

Interestingly enough, even the epitome of modern anti-Christianity, Friedrich Nietzsche, recognized the importance of Christianity as a complete belief structure for its truth claims, writing, "Christianity is a system, a view of things that is conceived as a connected whole. If you break off a major concept from it . . . you break up the whole as well: there are no necessities left to hold onto anymore."[120] Orr explains that whole systems of belief (in his day, secular, naturalistic modernity most especially) attacked the Christian faith from the angle of an entire belief system. Therefore, it is precisely at this level that the battle of beliefs occurs. As he later explains his methods (specifically for the lectures which spawned this work, but also for his apologetic approach in general),

> There is a definite Christian view of things, which has a character, coherence, and unity of its own, and stands in sharp contrast with counter theories and speculations, and that this world-view has the stamp of reason and reality upon itself, and can amply justify itself at the bar both of history and experience. I shall endeavour to show that the Christian view of things forms a logical whole which cannot be infringed on, or accepted or rejected piecemeal, but stands or falls in its integrity, and can only suffer from attempts at amalgamation or compromise with theories which rest on totally distinct bases. I hope thus to make clear at least the true nature of the issues involved in a comparison of the Christian and "modern" views, and I shall be glad if I can in any way contribute to the elucidation of the former.[121]

For Orr, Christianity alone made sense of the world and stood as an entire system.

The reason why defending Christianity as a worldview was so crucial to Orr is that he "realized that piecemeal responses to the worldviews of modernity were inadequate; what the time needed was a demonstration that Christianity was in itself a comprehensive vision of the whole of life."[122] Glen Scorgie explains that, for Orr, the "Christian view is tightly interconnected, and the smallest concession in any area would threaten the

119. Orr, *Christian View of God*, 3–4.
120. Nietzsche, *Twilight of the Idols*, 53.
121. Orr, *Christian View of God*, 16.
122. Bartholomew, *Contours of the Kuyperian Tradition*, 105.

entire edifice. The whole thing is vulnerable unless alertly defended at every point."[123] Moreover, for Orr, Christianity was worth defending because ultimately "it was the coherency of the Christian worldview, its harmony with reason and moral experience, that made it worthwhile."[124]

Abraham Kuyper

Abraham Kuyper joined Orr in this approach toward apologetics (although, as far as establishing a specific apologetic method, Kuyper took a different fork in the apologetic road). Kuyper notes that there is no doubt that "Christianity is imperiled by great and serious dangers," and believed that there were two life systems (the worldviews of Christianity and modernism) "wrestling one with another, in mortal combat."[125] James Edward McGoldrick further elaborates, stating,

> For [Kuyper] the manner in which people regard God, themselves, and the universe stands as the crux of the battle between good and evil, a struggle in which the opposing forces have no common ground. The current term culture war would have served Kuyper well. In this engagement it will not do to reply to the enemies' attacks in a piecemeal manner when two antithetical worldviews are locked in mortal combat. "Principle must be arrayed against principle," since a clash of life systems is in progress. Only Calvinism has the means to wage this struggle effectively. . . . The Reformed faith alone provides a comprehensive system embracing man's relation to God, to other men, and to the world.[126]

Kuyper lamented, though, that the apologetic endeavor did not make any headway in meeting the problem—the old ways and methods of Christian apologetics were no longer effective tools in fighting the battle. As McGoldrick asserts, "Kuyper contended that traditional defenses of particular doctrines could not avail in this struggle. Only the full-orbed worldview, which Calvinism alone can produce, could be effective. He knew learned modernists presented their views in logical, coherent arguments based on their axiomatic principles, so Christians must do nothing less."[127] Therefore,

---

123. Scorgie, *A Call for Continuity*, 54.

124. Scorgie, *A Call for Continuity*, 49.

125. Kuyper, *Calvinism*, 3–4.

126. McGoldrick, "Claiming Every Inch," 37.

127. McGoldrick, "Claiming Every Inch," 39.

Kuyper opines, "If the battle is to be fought with honour and with a hope of victory, then *principle* must be arrayed against *principle*; then it must be felt that in Modernism the vast energy of an all-embracing *life-system* assails us, then also it must be understood that we have to take our stand in a life-system of equally comprehensive and far-reaching power. And this powerful life-system is not to be invented nor formulated by ourselves, but is to be taken and applied as it presents itself in history. When thus taken, I found and confessed, and I still hold, that this manifestation of the Christian principle is given us in *Calvinism*."[128] Just as the entire life-system of modernity attacked Christianity, in response, his apologetic was the defense of Christianity as an all-embracing life-system.

Kuyper's treatment of apologetics and worldview differed from Orr in that he clearly rejected the autonomy of reason. While Orr and others attempted to meet their opponents on common epistemological ground, Kuyper saw too much antithesis between the believer and unbeliever. An unbeliever's epistemological foundation itself is a development of their worldview, which is too far removed from the Christian worldview. Thus, he laid the groundwork for what would become presuppositional apologetics.

Gordon H. Clark

Although Gordon H. Clark's contribution to worldview apologetics is not as prolific as Orr or Kuyper, he does bridge the philosophical and theological gap between Orr and Kuyper on the one hand and, on the other hand, those who would later expand upon this approach in the late twentieth century into the twenty-first century. Better known as a philosopher than an apologist, he nevertheless recognized the scope of apologetics as being a defense of an ordered system. Although he did not necessarily utilize the term "worldview," his description of Christianity as a rational system naturally leads to the concept itself. In a lengthy yet vitally important quote and contribution to the discussion, Clark explains,

> The macrocosmic world with its microcosmic but thoughtful inhabitant will not be a fortuitous aggregation of unrelated elements. Instead of a series of disconnected propositions, truth will be a rational system, a logically ordered series. . . . And each part will derive its significance from the whole. Christianity therefore has, or, one may even say, Christianity *is* a comprehensive view

128. Kuyper, *Calvinism*, 4–5. Emphasis original.

of all things: it takes the world, both material and spiritual, to be an ordered system. Consequently, if Christianity is to be defended against the objections of other philosophies, the only adequate method will be comprehensive. While it is of great importance to defend particular points of special interest, these specific defenses will be insufficient. In addition to these details, there is also needed a picture of the whole into which they fit. This comprehensive apologia is seen all the more clearly to be necessary as the contrasting theories are more carefully considered. The naturalistic philosophy that engulfs the modern minds is not a repudiation of one or two items of the Christian faith leaving the remainder untouched; it is not a philosophy that is satisfied to deny miracles while approving or at least not disapproving of Christian moral standards; on the contrary both Christianity and naturalism demand all or nothing: compromise is impossible. At least this will be true if the answer of any one question is integral with the answers of every other. Each system proposes to interpret all the facts; each system subscribes to the principle that this is one world. A *universe* . . . cannot exist half theistic and half atheistic. Politics, science, and epistemology must all be one or the other.[129]

Here, Clark notes that one does not find the truth scattered across the cosmos at various times in various places. Instead, the truth is an entire system that entails all of existence in every era. Therefore, only a worldview (a comprehensive view of all things) that reflects the truth itself could one call "true." That being the case, contradictory worldviews cannot all be true, and one must reject worldviews that embrace any hint of falsity (even if making many valid claims). Merely defending or attacking particular points of a system of thought is insufficient—certain points may be valid, yet the whole system itself is unsound. As Clark maintained, each worldview claims to interpret the facts correctly (and every single system does not do this and cannot do this); therefore, the systems themselves are scrutinized, and the one left standing embraces the entire system of truth.

Francis Schaeffer

Francis Schaeffer's theology and apologetic method are difficult to condense or summarize. At times he used the term "presupposition" synonymously with and in the place of "worldview," and yet the way he utilized presupposition in apologetics (in contrast to the way others such as Cornelius Van

129. Clark, *Christian View of Men*, 24–25. Emphasis original.

Til used the concept) has caused considerable confusion in describing and analyzing his work. Scott R. Burson and Jerry L. Walls note that the question of how to describe Schaeffer's apologetic methodology might be the most disputed and controversial subject about his life and ministry as they give a list of how other scholars describe his apologetic—some call him "presuppositionalist," others "compassionate presuppositionalist," still others say he is an "inconsistent presuppositionalist" or a "modified presuppositionalist," while others call him an "inconsistent empiricist," and others coined the term "verificationist" to describe him.[130] I contend that his work, no matter the label you may want to place on him, falls within the realm of worldview apologetics.

In defining his use of the term presupposition/worldview, Schaeffer states, "People have presuppositions, and they will live more consistently on the basis of these presuppositions than even they themselves may realize. By presuppositions we mean the basic way an individual looks at life, his basic world-view, the grid through which he sees the world. Presuppositions rest upon that which a person considers to be the truth of what exists. People's presuppositions lay a grid for all they bring forth into the external world. Their presuppositions also provide the basis for their values and therefore the basis for their decisions."[131] Although people may not know they have presuppositions, and may not understand that they have received their presuppositions from their family or society, it is possible to think about and analyze those presuppositions to see if they fit the facts or reality.[132] People function based on their presuppositions, and the presuppositions of Western society so radically shifted in Schaeffer's day that the change it caused within culture was substantial. However, the new presuppositions (and the culture built upon them) were false. Thus, for Schaeffer, a presupposition (a worldview) "must be subjected to the process of verification if we are to honestly discern their truth value."[133] That it is possible to compare and contrast worldviews and test for truthfulness is because (Schaeffer believed) Christians and non-Christians had common ground in that everyone lived in God's world, and without said common ground, conversation and communication would be impossible.[134] That worldviews

130. Burson and Walls, *Lewis & Schaeffer*, 143.

131. Schaeffer, *How Should We Then Live?*, 83.

132. Schaeffer, *He Is There*, 326.

133. Burson and Walls, *Lewis & Schaeffer*, 149.

134. Schaeffer, *The God Who Is There*, 138.

were testable was of the utmost importance because the "problem is having, and then acting upon the right world-view—the world-view which gives men and women the truth of what is."[135]

Schaeffer lamented that apologetics, up to his day, had never considered defending the faith from the scope of presupposition/worldview. He believed that the old apologetic methodologies were no longer effective in meeting the challenges of the modern day. Schaeffer explains why this is the case, writing, "The use of classical apologetics before this shift took place [in the conception of the way we come to knowledge and truth] was effective only because non-Christians were functioning, on the surface, on the same presuppositions, even if they had an inadequate base for them. In classical apologetics though, presuppositions were rarely analyzed, discussed or taken into account."[136] The belief that the Western world shares the same worldview is no longer viable. There is a great divide in presuppositions. Therefore, for Schaeffer, one tests presuppositions/worldviews for truthfulness because they cannot all accurately reflect reality since they are all contradictory.

Burson and Walls describe how and why worldviews are open to testing according to Schaeffer's thought when they write,

> Christianity, particularly the content of Scripture, should be subject to the same type of empirical inquiry as all other types of phenomena. Scientific, historical and religious claims all play by the same rules. For a theory in any of these disciplines to be viable it must be self-consistent, comprehensive and livable. Schaeffer insisted that religious truth be held to the same standard as scientific truth in light of the modern tendency to relegate religion to the realm of unverifiable. . . . Christianity is grounded in the claim that it is a true, historical, space-time religion and therefore open to verification and falsification.[137]

For a worldview to be a system making a truth claim, one must subject it to a verification process to discern the system's truth-value. Schaeffer said that one need not blindly accept the biblical system (or any other system)—it is verifiable.

Moreover, Schaeffer's description of the method is similar to the abductive logic discussed in the next chapter in that one takes the world's

135. Schaeffer, *How Should We Then Live?*, 252.

136. Schaeffer, *The God Who Is There*, 7.

137. Burson and Walls, *Lewis & Schaeffer*, 145.

truths and determines which system gives the best explanation for everything. Alternatively, he pictured it as "like trying to find the right key to fit a particular lock. We try the first key and then the next and the next until finally, if we are fortunate, one of them fits. The same principle applies (so Christians maintain) when we consider the big questions. Here are the phenomena. What key unlocks their meaning? What explanation is correct?"[138] Upon reviewing Schaeffer's work, I believe he built upon Orr and Kuyper's foundation in recognizing the need to test at the worldview level and laid the groundwork for future scholarly study.

Conclusion—Why Worldview for Apologetics?

Having described the history of the concept of worldview in philosophy and religion, having defined worldview in a manner that encompasses its significant features, and having demonstrated historical and current apologetic movements using worldview, one can understand how worldview is an effective scope from which to perform the apologetic task. The greatest reasoning for coming to apologetics from this perspective is the inescapability and importance of worldview. Although discussion about worldview is somewhat recent in history, this does not mean worldviews never existed. By analogy, just because a fossil lay dormant for thousands of years until found does not mean that the fossil had no existence until its discovery. Since the creation of man, humanity has possessed a systematic belief structure by which they interpreted the reality around them and by which they then made life decisions. Humanity may not have given it much thought, and they may not consciously look at reality through their worldview; nevertheless, it is through their worldview that they interpret what goes on around them and make their choices. It is a person's worldview that determines their philosophy of life, their religion, or their mission and vision. Whatever drives a person to do what they do, think what they think, believe what they believe, and be what they are, comes through their worldview. Since a person lives out of their belief structure, it only makes sense to test the truthfulness of the entirety of that system. Otherwise, their life is based on a lie.

Besides, from a Christian apologetic perspective, scholarly attacks on Christianity often (though not exclusively) take the form of attacking it as an overall system of belief rather than nitpicking at single doctrines or

138. Schaeffer and Koop, *Whatever Happened to the Human Race?*, 359.

ideas. Even if someone brings an attack against a solitary belief belonging to Christianity, it is more fruitful to demonstrate that the entire system is sound rather than try to parry each small argument. Moreover, in the realm of negative apologetics, where one deems to demonstrate the falseness of another worldview, it is much more effective to show that the entire system is unsound and cannot stand up to serious inquiry. To use an old fable as an analogy—if a Dutch dike represents a worldview, and each minor attack against single worldview beliefs is like poking a hole in the dike, it is much more helpful just to take out the entire dike rather than to poke little holes that the opponent can fix by sticking a finger in it (giving counter-arguments to every single critique).

Also, apologetics from the scope of worldview is most effective against the effects of globalization and pluralization. Modern technology and the ease of mobility for humanity expose people to every conceivable worldview and philosophical idea. When putting faces to the worldview (through personal acquaintance and relationship that they have with friends, neighbors, coworkers, or schoolmates), it grows more challenging to denounce anyone's belief system as wrong—thus the growing hostility toward exclusive truth claims. Worldview apologetics conclusively demonstrates that different worldviews make contradicting claims that cannot all be true (no matter any claim to the contrary) and gives a way of testing the worldviews, so people may objectively see which is true and which is false.

Finally, apologetics from the scope of worldview effectively combats the effects of postmodernism, including its influence on those who would do away with the apologetic task altogether. Although postmodernism is difficult to define, it is noticeable by its skepticism toward objective truth and metanarratives—a view that has even crept into some circles of Christianity. Worldview apologetics demonstrates that postmodernism itself is a worldview—a systematic belief structure expressed as a metanarrative—that one can test for truthfulness even though it denies the existence of metanarratives. Since its truth claims contradict claims made by Christianity, testing said claims is a legitimate endeavor to keep people from error and lead them to the truth.

Having argued for apologetics within the scope of worldviews, I then ask what is the most effective means of testing the truthfulness of these various belief structures? I argue that an abductive use of epistemological tests for truth in the realm of major life questions successfully demonstrates the truth or falsity of systematic belief systems.

3

Weighing the Evidence through Abductive Reasoning

"'It's abductive reasoning, not deductive. Working from observation to theory
is abduction, not deduction.' 'But I thought—' 'Yes, you and so many other
people. We know who to blame, of course, and I've written to [Arthur Conan
Doyle] more than once [in] care of his publisher, but he takes no notice.'"

—T.E. KINSEY, *A Quiet Life in the Country*

IN HIS DISSERTATION ENTITLED "Evangelical Worldview Analysis: A Critical
Assessment and Proposal," Bryan Billard Sims notes that Evangelical
Christians use two primary methodologies to analyze, compare, and contrast worldviews—transcendental analysis and abductive reasoning.[1] He
reveals that the transcendental argument "states that the Christian worldview as revealed in Scripture is the necessary precondition for knowledge,
ethics, metaphysics, and meaning. Any other starting point ends in self-contradiction or absurdity."[2] Sims finds the transcendental argument wanting
as there remains an inability to "provide an indubitable argument that will
bridge the chasm between conceptual and ontological necessity as well as

1. Sims, "Evangelical Worldview Analysis," 21.
2. Sims, "Evangelical Worldview Analysis," 25.

categorically rule out alternative worldviews, particularly concrete theistic worldviews as well as hypothetical ones."[3] He also remarks that the strong claim of transcendentalists about the divine self-attestation of Scripture and the claim that absolute certainty is obtainable are without merit.[4] Sims found too many challenges with the transcendental analysis of worldviews, so he claims that the abductive analysis of worldviews is the stronger option.

Sims describes abductive reasoning, often referred to as "inference to the best explanation," as "the pattern of arguing backward from some phenomenon to its cause or explanation."[5] As noted below, abductive reasoning has experienced a resurgence of application in several other fields with much success. As numerous Christian apologists have begun to appropriate this approach for defending the Christian faith, Sims finds this method the best for worldview analysis for four reasons. First, it is a prevalent mode of reasoning in ordinary life and specialized disciplines. Second, it taps into a broad spectrum of evidence and fields. Third, having a wide range of evidence, arguments, and phenomena to choose from removes the burden of producing one singular decisive argument. Finally, abductive reasoning follows the contours of human thinking with regard to worldviews.[6]

I agree with Sims' assessment, although I find a different set of criteria for abductive reasoning's use more compelling. This chapter first defines abductive reasoning and contrasts it with other logical argumentations. It then discusses the philosophical roots of abductive reasoning to lay a foundation to comprehend its use. Next, this chapter briefly explores how other scholarly fields have used abductive reasoning to demonstrate its adaptability for other such practices like apologetics. Then it considers abduction's suitability for Christian apologetics and seeks to establish its strengths as a method for the defense of the faith. This chapter surveys various criticisms and explores defeaters raised against abduction's conclusions and then answers these criticisms to further strengthen abduction's application to worldview apologetics. The chapter concludes by discussing criteria for abductive considerations and determining abduction's place in worldview truth-testing.

3. Sims, "Evangelical Worldview Analysis," 70.

4. Sims, "Evangelical Worldview Analysis," 70.

5. Sims, "Evangelical Worldview Analysis," 71.

6. Sims, "Evangelical Worldview Analysis," 97–98.

Abductive Reasoning among the Other Logics

When considering logical reasoning, the two most prominent types of arguments are deductive and inductive. Often given in a syllogistic form, deduction demonstrates that a relationship exists between two (or more) premises which draw a conclusion that must certainly be true.[7] Deduction, proceeding from the general to the particular, draws consequences that are necessary if the premises themselves are true.[8] Norman L. Geisler and Ronald M. Brooks define a deductive argument as one "where (if valid) the conclusion follows necessarily from the premises; arguing from a general concept to a particular situation."[9] So, for example, a deductive argument might state that if all A's are B's, and all B's are C's, then all A's are C's. However, as Sims notes, deduction is tautological in that it never says anything more than what the premises assumed from the beginning, so it does not yield any new information.[10] Yet, deduction is helpful in that it demonstrates that premises one accepts as true often yield conclusions that (logically speaking) must be true (but, possibly, one may not have previously accepted without the deductive process).

Induction, on the other hand, proceeds from the particular to the general, drawing an inference from observed frequencies of an occurrence.[11] The conclusion does not follow directly from the premises, but the premises support the conclusion and render it probable.[12] Unlike deduction, an inductive inference does not lead to a necessary conclusion but only a probable truth.[13] For example, an inductive argument might note that every time one observes an A, it has the quality of B; therefore, it is highly probable that the next A one observes will also have the quality of B (although one cannot say this with absolute certainty).

There is another way to come to a warranted logical conclusion without it being "entailed by one's premises" or "derived from the evidence by inductive extrapolation."[14] Abductive reasoning (sometimes simply called

7. Aliseda, "Mathematical Reasoning vs. Abductive Reasoning," 25.

8. Groothuis, *Christian Apologetics*, 435.

9. Geisler and Brooks, *Come, Let Us Reason*, 189.

10. Sims, "Evangelical Worldview Analysis," 74.

11. Douven, "Abduction," 4–5. See also Geisler and Brooks, *Come, Let Us Reason*, 191.

12. Cohen, "Induction," 405.

13. Samples, *Without a Doubt*, 109.

14. Wainwright, *Philosophy of Religion*, 166.

abduction) infers from the given data and premises to form or choose a hypothesis that best explains the given information.[15] John R. and Susan G. Josephson describe abductive reasoning as finding the most plausible composite hypothesis made from numerous sub-hypotheses, which then can explain all the data.[16] C. J. Hookway explains this type of reasoning as accepting "a conclusion on the grounds that it explains the available evidence."[17] Lorenzo Magnani defines abduction as "the process of *inferring* certain facts and/or laws and hypotheses that render some sentences plausible, that *explain* or *discover* some (eventually new) phenomenon or observation: it is the process of reasoning in which explanatory hypotheses are formed and evaluated."[18] For these reasons, abductive reasoning is often termed "inference to the best explanation." Many view abduction as related to induction in that they both only lead to merely probable inferences, and both are defeasible, meaning further data could refute their conclusions.[19] However, abduction and induction are distinct in that abduction "appears as the path from facts towards ideas and theories, while induction is the path from ideas and theories towards facts in order to obtain a basis for statistical assessment of the ideas' and theories' probabilities."[20] Another way of observing the contrast is that abduction provides the best broad explanatory hypothesis for the data, while induction attempts to predict specific probable outcomes from what one observed in the data.[21] Nevertheless, the three forms of logic have interacting purposes: "Abduction generates a new hypothesis, deduction draws the consequences and induction examines them within our social reality."[22] To give an example of how induction and abduction are inverses of deduction and to demonstrate their differences, Charles Sanders Peirce (the philosophical father of abduction) provides the following illustration:

15. Fann, *Peirce's Theory of Abduction*, 5.

16. Josephson and Josephson, *Abductive Inference*, 178.

17. Hookway, "Abduction".

18. Magnani, "Abduction and Chance Discovery," 273. Emphasis original.

19. Aliseda, "Mathematical Reasoning vs. Abductive Reasoning," 25.

20. Hoffmann, "Problems with Peirce's Concept of Abduction," 272.

21. Samples, *A World of Difference*, 52.

22. Halas, "In Error We Trust," 704.

DEDUCTION:
Rule.—All the beans from this bag are white.
Case.—These beans are from this bag.
Result.—These beans are white.
INDUCTION:
Case.—These beans are from this bag.
Result.—These beans are white.
Rule.—All the beans from this bag are white
HYPOTHESIS [ABDUCTION]:
Rule.—All the beans from this bag are white.
Result.—These beans are white.
Case.—These beans are from this bag.[23]

As seen below, abductive reasoning can consider several deductive and inductive arguments taken together to lead to a concluding hypothesis.

Philosophical Roots of Abductive Reasoning

Philosophers grant that the concept of abductive reasoning has a long history in philosophical thought, some making a comparison with Aristotle's apagoge (an indirect argument that proves a point by demonstrating the absurdity of the opposite), others recognizing its reasoning from effects to cause in older works on scientific methodology, while still others see references to this form of reasoning in older works on logic.[24] However, pragmatist Charles Sanders Peirce gave abduction its name (after having evolved from previous monikers such as hypothesis or retroduction, among others) and gave substance to its current form and understanding. Scholars consider abduction a vital part of his pragmatist philosophy because Peirce viewed it as "an intermediary stage between perception and cognition."[25]

Despite its importance, scholars have encountered difficulties in systematizing Peirce's thoughts on abduction as there is no single definitive work that he wrote on the subject, and his ideas evolved and matured over time. In several places, Peirce indicated that abduction is a logic used to construct a hypothesis, "generating new theoretical discoveries."[26] Peirce specified elsewhere that it is a logic used in selecting one particular

23. Peirce, *Collected Papers*, 2:623.

24. Aliseda, *Abductive Reasoning*, 7; Walton, *Abductive Reasoning*, 22–23.

25. Khachab, "Logical Goodness of Abduction," 162.

26. McKaughan, "Ugly Duckling to Swan," 447.

hypothesis out of several possibilities, justifying the belief that one hypothesis is probably true as opposed to the others.[27] Yet still, some have also interpreted abduction as a path to determining if a particular hypothesis is worthy of pursuit—if a particular idea is promising or worthwhile.[28] It is in these latter two cases where I see abduction's most significant use in analyzing and evaluating worldviews. *The Oxford Companion to Philosophy* recognizes two varieties of inference emanating from abduction, stating, "In one sense, it is 'inference to the best explanation', which is a means of justifying the postulation of unobservable phenomena on the strength of explanations they afford of observable phenomena. In its other variety, abduction is the process of forming *generic* beliefs from known data. Observations incline us to think that tigers are four-legged, a proposition we hold true even upon discovery of a three-legged tiger. Generic sentences differ from general (i.e. universally quantified) sentences by their accommodation of negative instances, that is, of instances which would falsify general sentences."[29] Magnani recognizes two primary epistemological meanings for abduction: "1) abduction that only generates 'plausible' hypotheses ('selective' or 'creative') and 2) abduction considered as inference 'to the best explanation', which also evaluates hypotheses." He also maintains that there are two types of theoretical abduction: "'sentential', related to logic and to verbal/symbolic inferences, and 'model-based', related to the exploitation of internalized models of diagrams, pictures, etc."[30]

To understand if one or all of these purposes and interpretations of abduction are feasible, one must consider the general form Peirce gave of abductive inference:

> The surprising fact, C, is observed.
> But if A were true, C would be a matter of course.
> Hence, there is reason to suspect that A is true.[31]

Josephson and Josephson give abduction the following form, which seems like a more articulate explanation of the reasoning process:

---

27. Fann, *Peirce's Theory of Abduction*, 41; Frankfurt, "Peirce's Notion of Abduction," 593.

28. McKaughan, "Ugly Duckling to Swan," 452; Frankfurt, "Peirce's Notion of Abduction," 595.

29. "Inference," 407. Emphasis original.

30. Magnani, "Abduction and Chance Discovery," 273.

31. Peirce, *Collected Papers*, 5:189.

D is a collection of data.
H explains *D*.
No other hypothesis can explain *D* as well as *H* does.
Therefore, *H* is probably true.[32]

The form of abduction in either account allows for generating, choosing, or evaluating a hypothesis that accurately explains the premises, facts, or data provided. Peirce further described abduction as a reasoned inference (a perceptive judgment) and an appeal to instinct (an insight available to all humanity).[33] Not that these two are necessarily exclusive, for one could say that the formation of a hypothesis involves both logic and psychology.[34] Nevertheless, abduction is much more than merely an intelligent guess, for there is an underlying structure of causal, albeit informal, reasoning that leads one to a probable, sufficient conclusion.[35] Thereby, abduction has several promising uses, all beneficial for worldview analysis.

Contemporary Use of Abductive Reasoning

After Peirce laid the groundwork, abductive reasoning quickly became embedded in philosophy, especially epistemology and philosophy of science. However, several other scholarly fields found abduction to be a valuable tool in both theory and practice, with many picking up the mantle as abduction's effectiveness gained more significant notice. Considering abduction's adaptability to these fields demonstrates its adaptability for the apologetic endeavor.

General and Social Sciences

Peirce not only considered abduction a logical tool for philosophy but, more specifically, an instrument for scientific advancement. Peirce viewed abduction as the logical process that occurs before deduction and induction in any scientific argumentation, for abduction forms the hypothesis that deduction and induction later test.[36] As described by Cameron Shel-

---

32. Josephson and Josephson, *Abductive Inference*, 14.
33. Fann, *Peirce's Theory of Abduction*, 167.
34. Hoffmann, "Peirce's Concept of Abduction," 282.
35. Walton, *Abductive Reasoning*, 158–59.
36. Walton, *Abductive Reasoning*, 8.

ley, "Peirce came to view scientific investigations as proceeding in four stages: (1) observation of an anomaly, (2) abduction of hypotheses for the purpose of explaining the anomaly, (3) inductive testing of the hypotheses in experiments, and (4) deductive confirmation that the selected hypothesis does predict the original anomaly."[37] As such, some attribute several of the great scientific finds of the past to an abductive process that they would then later verify through inductive and deductive methods. For example, some attribute the discovery of Neptune as the eighth planet in our solar system to a work of abductive reasoning. Considering the evidence of why Uranus deviated from the orbit that astronomers predicted, they concluded that the best hypothesis to explain the data was the influence of another planet. They then confirmed the hypothesis through later testing.[38]

Paul Thagard notes that "philosophers of science have recognized the importance of abduction in the discovery and evaluation of scientific theories, and researchers in artificial intelligence have realized that abduction is a key part . . . [in] tasks that require finding explanations."[39] Of course, scientists may put forth any hypothesis that appears to deal with the data adequately, but this hypothesis must be verifiable and pass tests of truth to determine its accuracy. For example, Charles Darwin observed the distribution of species and the existence of atrophied organs and abductively hypothesized natural selection, reasoning, "It can hardly be supposed that a false theory would explain, in so satisfactory a manner as does the theory of natural selection, the several large classes of facts above specified. It has recently been objected that this is an unsafe method of arguing; but it is a method used in judging of the common events of life, and has often been used by the greatest natural philosophers. The undulatory theory of light has thus been arrived at; and the belief in the revolution of the earth on its own axis was until lately supported by hardly any direct evidence. It is no valid objection that science as yet throws no light on the far higher problem of the essence or origin of life."[40] Darwin thought that since everyday events and significant scientific findings came about through abduction, his use was sound. He may have used the logic correctly, but the hypothesis that he posited has yet to receive verification; it has many problems passing tests of truth of empirical adequacy, and it is unable to answer defeaters placed

---

37. Shelley, "Visual Abductive Reasoning," 279.

38. Douven, "Abduction," 7.

39. Thagard, Foreword to *Abduction, Reason, and Science*, ix.

40. Darwin, *The Origin of Species*, 239.

against it (e.g., lack of fossil evidence or consideration of better alternative hypotheses such as irreducible complexity).

One can find an example of a practical scientific use of abduction within the medical profession. A medical specialist observes the symptoms that the patient displays as well as listens to clues given by the patient through their "History of Present Illness"—their testimony of what they have experienced, the time frame involved, the relationship between symptoms, and their personal interpretation of what has happened.[41] Then, based on the accumulation of that data, the medical professional creates a hypothesis that gives a causal relation between symptoms and disease.[42] They next confirm the hypothesis through testing. Many medical scholars now recognize the advantages of abduction as a first step in the health care process. As one scholar states, "The holistic approach of abductive reasoning can allow nursing students (and students of other health disciplines) to build hypotheses through maximum data retrieval and to develop causal models that illustrate and explain the underlying structures of the situation."[43] Such a diverse use of abduction in science demonstrates its adaptability to other disciplines (including Christian apologetics). Science, however, is not the only area of scholarship that has recently plumbed the depths of the advantages of abductive reasoning.

Law

Legal experts have recognized abduction's broad use and essential effects in their discipline. Several areas of the legal system employ abductive reasoning first to infer possible explanations for what occurred in a particular case and then to determine which of those explanations makes the best hypothesis given the evidence. As Giovanni Tuzet defines it, "Legal abduction is the inference which goes from an effect, legally relevant, to its cause, providing for the *best explanation* of the known effect."[44] For example, the detectives of a criminal case consider all the evidence and witness interviews they collect, list the possible explanations that take all of them into account, and finally choose the one hypothesis that gives the most reasonable

41. Schleifer and Vannatta, "The Logic of Diagnosis," 364.

42. Aliseda, *Abductive Reasoning*, 7.

43. Mirza et al., "Concept Analysis of Abductive Reasoning," 1990.

44. Tuzet, "Legal Abduction," 43. Emphasis original.

conclusion in light of all the data.[45] One may think of the fantastic skills attributed to fictional detective Sherlock Holmes who was a genius at inventing hypotheses. All too often, his skills are wrongfully ascribed to great deductive prowess. However, the fictional hero would describe a process of reasoning backward, showing himself a master of abduction rather than deduction (hence, the quote in this chapter's epigraph).

Abduction plays a vital role in the courtroom as well. Jurors use abduction to incorporate witness testimony and the other data given as evidence and then evaluate whether to accept or reject the testimony presented.[46] Some scholars believe that jurors use abduction to fill in the gaps with assumed hypotheses, where some essential knowledge is incomplete, to come to the most reasonable conclusion of what the court proceedings presented them.[47] Thus, not only do jurors consider the content and quality of arguments and evidence presented, but they can also envision other causal possibilities in rendering their verdicts.[48]

Use and Strengths in Christian Apologetics

Considering the broad use of abductive reasoning in other fields of scholarship, it is not a reach to deem it a valuable tool in the hands of the Christian apologist. Doctors give their abductively-formed prognosis (their best explanation or hypothesis) based on symptoms and data from medical tests, and police abductively conclude who the culprit is based on collected evidence. Similarly, a Christian apologist puts forth the Christian worldview as the hypothesis that gives the best explanation of the state of the universe based on the data. With an increased acknowledgment of its usefulness, I see abductive logic as having birthed two recognized ways of defending Christianity and disproving opposing worldviews.

45. Wallace, *Cold-Case Christianity*, sect. 1, chap. 2, no page nos., Logos Bible Software.

46. Adler, "Testimony, Trust, Knowing," 275.

47. Ciampolini and Torroni, "Using Abductive Logic Agents," 253–54.

48. Green and McCloy, "Reaching a Verdict," 330.

Cumulative Case Apologetics as an Abductive Methodology

An effective use of abductive reasoning in the apologetic task is to take given arguments, facts, evidence, and data and demonstrate how the hypothesis of God (or some specific belief or doctrine within Christianity) best explains those premises. Cumulative case apologetics seeks to demonstrate how Christianity explains the evidence and available data.

Basil Mitchell first gave this apologetic approach (although not necessarily new as a method) its current form and name. He noted at the time that there appeared to be two assumptions regarding philosophical considerations of Christianity. On the one hand, some assume it is impossible to prove Christian theism. On the other hand, neither can critics show Christianity as false or logically incoherent. For Mitchell, this left only two alternatives: either "there can be no rational case for or against Christianity," or "the case [for Christianity] must be a cumulative one which is rational, but does not take the form of a strict proof or argument from probability."[49] This method has logic and reasonableness, for "the basic idea is that a rational or reasonable case can be made out for a position by the patient accumulation of various pieces of evidence."[50]

The beauty of the method is that it can take pieces of evidence that individually do not have the strength to make the explicit claim for a transcendent Being (or some other doctrine) but then join them together to build the case toward a single hypothesis.[51] For Christian apologetics especially, one can contend that the traditional arguments (such as the cosmological argument, the teleological argument, and moral argument) in and of themselves do not succeed as necessary proofs for Christian truths.[52] However, when one places the arguments together as individual premises pointing toward a specific hypothesis, they carry weight in an overall defense.

The cumulative case method fits within the scope of abductive reasoning in that (just as was mentioned with Peirce's treatments of the matter) the Christian apologist is now "urging that traditional theism makes better sense of all the evidence available than does any alternative on offer."[53] In other words, the most viable hypothesis is Christian the-

---

49. Mitchell, *Justification of Religious Belief*, 39.

50. Abraham, "Cumulative Case Arguments," 19.

51. Mitchell, *Justification of Religious Belief*, 40–41.

52. Feinberg, *Can You Believe It's True?* 321.

53. Mitchell, *Justification of Religious Belief*, 40.

ism, considering the accumulation of various proofs and arguments. As Paul D. Feinberg summarizes this method, what "Christian apologists are defending is the claim that Christian theism is the best explanation of all available evidence on offer. The opponents are required to present a more convincing cumulative case."[54]

With the abductive reasoning found in cumulative case apologetics, there is a freedom and openness for the defender of the faith. Apologists can use premises or arguments with various forms, content, and structure (deductive or inductive, empirical or non-empirical, formal or informal, quantifiable or non-quantifiable).[55] From cosmological to biological to historical to logical evidence, an array of data from various fields strengthen Christian conclusions. Several apologists have utilized this method to lead to specific theological hypotheses, three of which I give as examples to demonstrate abduction at work in this form of cumulative case apologetics. While the following are examples of positive apologetics, one may also use abductive reasoning in negative apologetics.

The Existence of God

One of the central questions in philosophy is whether a transcendent, supernatural Being called God exists. Many theologians in the past have used logical and philosophical arguments, often in deductive form, claiming that their singular case gives near definitive proof for the existence of God (for example, Anselm's ontological argument, William Paley's teleological argument, William Lane Craig's Kalam cosmological argument). Several philosophers in history have identified weaknesses in these solitary arguments, bringing into question the strength of their conclusion. However, suppose one would take each argument as a single piece of evidence within an overall case after considering all such premises. In that case, the logically best explanation to which they together infer is that a supernatural God exists. What one argues is that out of all the possible hypotheses that could explain the evidence, the best hypothesis is the Christian God.

An excellent example is Richard Swinburne's work *The Existence of God*. Swinburne does not himself use the term abduction, instead describing various forms of inductive argument. Nevertheless, one could argue that the manner in which he came to his conclusion is abductive. Swinburne

54. Feinberg, "Cumulative Case Apologetics," 152.

55. Abraham, "Cumulative Case Arguments," 20.

lays out numerous individual arguments, each of which he believes is more probable if there is a God than if there is not a God.[56] He outlines the cosmological argument (chap. 7), teleological argument (chap. 8), arguments from consciousness and morality (chap. 9), arguments from providence (chap. 10), arguments from history and miracles (chap. 11), and arguments from religious experience (chap. 13). After discussing the strengths of each argument and the probability for theism given each one, he then considers their totality and concludes, "On our total evidence theism is more probable than not," and adds the note that if "the detailed historical evidence of the life, death, and Resurrection of Jesus" are also taken into account, then "the probability that there is a God becomes very much greater than that."[57] Thus, given the totality of each argument as an individual premise, Swinburne determines that the hypothesis that gives the best explanation is "that there is a God who made and sustains man and the universe."[58]

Creation

Not only can accumulated evidence lead to the overall explanation of God's existence, but various arguments and premises can abductively demonstrate specific Christian doctrines. For example, abductive reasoning can lead to the hypothesis that the universe is a unique creation of a supernatural Being. At least one scientist admits that "the same reasoning process that scientists use, day in and day out, to evaluate a hypothesis rationally and logically leads to the expectation that life, at its most fundamental level, stemmed from a Creator's handiwork."[59] Thus, if one considers the evidence and arguments of the likelihood that the universe had a beginning (cosmological argument), that the universe reflects design in various ways, including fine-tuning (teleological argument), that the universe is capable of rational investigation, that there is much to consider by way of the fossil evidence, as well as taking into account the complexity of DNA, one must consider that these together point to "an intelligent designer rather than undirected time and chance."[60] While several philosophers and scientists have abductively concluded that natural evolutionary forces explain the

56. Swinburne, *The Existence of God*, 278.
57. Swinburne, *The Existence of God*, 342.
58. Swinburne, *The Existence of God*, 342.
59. Rana, *The Cell's Design*, 277.
60. Markos, "Debating Design," 10.

universe and humanity, others admit that, given the cumulative effect of the evidence, an intelligent designer offers a better explanation.

Christ's Resurrection

Another theological belief often reasoned through abduction is the resurrection of Christ. Gary Habermas recognizes that many secular historians and philosophers will reject certain types of arguments and pieces of evidence, so he uses a "minimal facts approach" in which the only data considered in the abductive process is that which is well-evidenced and accepted by most secular scholars.[61] Under this approach, Habermas considers numerous points of fact:

> (1) Jesus died by crucifixion and (2) was buried. (3) Jesus' death caused the disciples to despair and lose hope, believing that his life was ended. (4) Although not as widely accepted, many scholars hold that the tomb in which Jesus was buried was discovered to be empty just a few days later. Critical scholars further agree that (5) the disciples had experiences which they believed were literal appearances of the risen Jesus. Because of these experiences, (6) the disciples were transformed from doubters who were afraid to identify themselves with Jesus to bold proclaimers of his death and resurrection. (7) This message was the center of preaching in the early church and (8) was especially proclaimed in Jerusalem, where Jesus died and was buried shortly before. As a result of this preaching, (9) the church was born and grew, (10) with Sunday as the primary day of worship. (11) James, who had been a skeptic, was converted to the faith when he also believed that he saw the resurrected Jesus. (12) A few years later, Paul was converted by an experience which he, likewise, believed to be an appearance of the risen Jesus.[62]

The hypothesis that gives the best explanation of all this evidence is that Jesus Christ bodily rose from the dead.

While the cumulative case approach, as commonly described, supports various Christian conclusions and makes Christianity more probable, it does not necessarily uphold Christianity as an entire system of belief, nor does it necessarily falsify opposing worldviews as belief structures that go against truth claims. Of course, this may be nitpicky, but one could argue

61. Habermas and Licona, *Case for the Resurrection*, loc. 337–41, Kindle.
62. Habermas, *The Historical Jesus*, 158.

for a difference between the standard understanding of cumulative case apologetics and what I am proposing. For what I see Sims proposing, and what I see in the works of others, is that apologists can use abduction to evaluate the truthfulness of an entire worldview system.

Abductive Reasoning, Worldview Analysis, and Truth

Abductive reasoning is the logical means of worldview selection and assessment for apologetics. Walton recognizes both theory generation and evaluation as "two components of abduction that represent two different tasks undertaken during the execution of abductive reasoning."[63] So, not only does one use abduction to create the hypothesis (choose or generate a worldview to make sense of the data of life), one then uses abduction to evaluate or verify the hypothesis given (test the veracity of a worldview). One can consider worldviews to be the hypotheses people form to explain reality. William Hasker observes that worldviews "function for us in ways that are similar, though not identical, to the functioning of scientific theories; they serve to unify areas of our experience and make them understandable to us."[64]

Some evangelicals may take offense to the treatment of the Christian worldview simply as a considered hypothesis since it is no mere religion but a relationship with the living God. However, one must first consider that those who do not share the Christian worldview do not have that same attitude or reverence toward the faith, so for them, the faith is nothing more than a mere possibility at best. Secondly, a worldview (in a sense) is a hypothesis in that it provides a broad-ranging theory of everything, trying to account for the nature and meaning of the universe (the data of arguments and evidence).[65] An abductive worldview analysis starts with tentative hypotheses from experience and then, through a method of verification, subject the hypotheses to testing and confirmation (or disconfirmation) by the coherence of their account with the relevant lines of data.[66]

For worldview apologetics, the apologist takes the data and evidence given in the world and demonstrates how and why their hypothesis or belief structure best explains that which exists. As Arlie J. Hoover explains,

---

63. Walton, *Abductive Reasoning*, 22.

64. Hasker, *Metaphysics*, 25–26.

65. Groothuis, *Christian Apologetics*, 49–50.

66. Burson and Walls, *Lewis & Schaeffer*, 142–43.

"A good worldview is established, not by one line of evidence, or by one knock-out argument, but by cumulative evidence by converging lines from several sources of data. A skillful metaphysician builds up his case by showing that his theory explains material from several divergent sources. Like the separate strands of a rope, his converging lines of evidence combine to strengthen the central theory. The view that has the most strands, other things being equal, is the strongest view."[67]

The Christian apologist presents the Christian worldview as the most cogent view, given the converging lines of evidence. As Paul Feinberg describes, "Traditional Christian theists are urging that their explanation makes better sense of all the evidence available than does any other alternative worldview on offer, whether that alternative is some other theistic view or atheism. The opponent is contesting that claim."[68] Then, also abductively, the apologist evaluates their worldview and opposing worldviews for truthfulness according to assured criteria of testing. One then rejects any hypothesis/worldview that does not hold up to these collective tests of truthfulness. As William Wainwright summarizes, "Attempts to show that a worldview is superior to its rivals are inferences to the best explanation, and . . . the criteria for assessing these explanations are, for the most part, those used in assessing any explanatory hypothesis."[69] I argue in the next chapter that, based on current worldview apologetic trends, the criteria for assessing the explanatory hypotheses (worldviews) are three truth-tests based on a combined effort of the three major epistemological theories of truth.

Alex McLellan's metaphorical picture gives an astute analogy to this abductive approach where he likens worldview hypothesizing and evaluation to a jigsaw puzzle.[70] The universe is composed of numerous pieces that, when put together, make a whole picture of reality. Unfortunately, unlike a real jigsaw puzzle, no box displays the picture of how the puzzle ought to look. So, a person must begin somewhat blindly attempting to put the picture together. However, putting the puzzle together is possible because there are corner and edge pieces where one can begin—the basic building blocks of life to which one can add other pieces. The more pieces that a person fits together, the better hypothesis/worldview they can make of what the whole of the picture is most likely to be (the abductive reasoning

67. Hoover, *Dear Agnos*, 51–52.

68. Feinberg, "Cumulative Case Apologetics," 152.

69. William J. Wainwright, "Worldviews," 87.

70. McLellan, *A Jigsaw Guide*.

process). The hypothesis/worldview that best explains all the pieces and can continue to fit the remaining pieces rightly has the strongest support. However, many hypotheses/worldviews attempt to make sense of the puzzle, and they contradict one another in such a way that they all cannot be true (one person may say the puzzle is a picture of a dog and another a picture of a flower). So, there are ways to abductively test if a hypothesis/worldview accurately explains what puzzle pieces have already been placed together, whether it can account for the remaining pieces, and whether it gives the best explanation of the picture that is forming.

Sims offers a three-step procedure for his version of abductive worldview analysis that summarizes how this worldview apologetic approaches the task. First, the Christian apologist and their opponent must find common features to human existence in order to dialogue; next both sides put forward their worldview as the best explanation of the data; finally, the Christian apologist contrasts their position with that of the opponent's.[71] Sims concludes that in the "final assessment, abductive analysis alone possesses the conceptual capacity to engage alternative worldviews."[72] While I agree that abduction has that capacity, what I find in current works of worldview apologists is that instead of contrasting worldview positions with one another, the apologist abductively evaluates proposed worldviews according to tests of truth based on the most common epistemological theories of truth in philosophy. Does a hypothesis/worldview meet the cumulative criteria of truth?

Analysis of Abduction in Apologetics

Abductive reasoning has many strengths as a tool in Christian apologetics. First, although logically it only leads to a probable explanation for the evidence, it is not mere guesswork but directs itself toward a rationally strong conclusion. Numerous criteria give credence to it as a method, such that when one infers Christian beliefs, they genuinely are logical extensions given the premises. Second, abduction is not bound to one particular form or structure in its argumentation. There is a freedom and flexibility in considering any relevant piece of evidence (be it deductive, inductive, or otherwise). No critical piece of information is excluded simply because it does not fit the mold of a specified argument. Third, abductive reasoning as

71. Sims, "Evangelical Worldview Analysis," 82.
72. Sims, "Evangelical Worldview Analysis," 115.

a method is flexible enough for use in accounting for any primary theological belief in Christianity and the Christian worldview as a whole. Abduction is not bound only to infer that God exists but also other central tenets of the faith. Whereas an argument such as the cosmological argument leads to the necessary idea of an Uncaused Cause, it can go no further. Abduction, however, can take into consideration the accumulation of all beliefs. However, as much as the method has various strengths, one must also consider whether abductive reasoning can hold its ground against assorted criticisms and defeaters.

Replying to Criticisms of Abductive Reasoning

Not everyone is enamored with abductive reasoning. Several detractors have raised logical and philosophical criticisms against it as a method. I briefly discuss a sample of such criticisms to determine if they are so powerful that they render abduction impotent as a philosophical tool, thereby demonstrating it to be ineffective for Christian apologetics.

Defense against Logical Fallacies

As a form of logic, abduction opens itself up to fallacies the same way deduction and induction do. Thus, a fallacy can neutralize the reasoning abduction attempts to convey. There are two specific fallacies that critics often accuse it of committing, thereby claiming any conclusion based on such methods is invalid.

False Alternatives Fallacy

Known by several other names (such as false dilemma fallacy and false choice fallacy), this fallacy argues that the one making a hypothesis considers too few alternative hypotheses. A philosopher may believe that only two or three hypotheses could explain the given premises, out of which one is the best explanation, but there are several more that he has not envisioned which could equally, or more likely, explain the given evidence.[73] Thus, all

---

73. Damer, *Attacking Faulty Reasoning*, 56–57; Kahane, *Logic and Contemporary Rhetoric*, 56–58.

the reasoned hypotheses may be wrong because one has not yet conceived the correct hypothesis.

Of course, taken to its extreme, one could feasibly say that the only way to avoid this fallacy is to consider every single possibility, which could go on infinitely and lead to absurdity. Although it is impossible to deal with every single conceivable alternative hypothesis, it is not irrational to expect the one conducting the abductive reasoning to have carefully considered several highly probable explanations. If the criteria considered in the next chapter have guided the process of creating, choosing, or evaluating hypotheses, it is ill-conceived to assume that someone has not considered enough explanations. Critics often charge Christian apologists with this fallacy, accusing them of merely presupposing a theistic hypothesis to the evidence without considering what the evidence reveals nor allowing themselves to consider alternative, non-theistic explanations. A Christian apologist must consider why the evidence does not point elsewhere and be able to give reasons why other hypotheses are unfounded and why the theistic hypothesis is the inference to the best explanation. The apologist should have considered and then refuted counterexamples, not presuming on one's preconceived notions.[74]

Post Hoc Fallacy

A post hoc fallacy occurs when an argument (according to critics) unjustifiably concludes that one event caused another event just because there is some connection or positive correlation between the two.[75] For example, I notice that every time I wear my favorite sports team's baseball cap, my favorite team wins, but every time I do not wear my favorite team's baseball cap, my team loses. Therefore, I conclude that my cap-wearing determined the outcome of the games. I observed the correlation, and I reason that one causes the other.

Critics claim that abductive reasoning lends itself to this fallacy. They argue that merely because a hypothesis explains the given premises does not necessarily mean that there is some causal relationship. The correlation could simply be a strange coincidence. Still, it would seem presumptuous to deny a causal relationship between premises and explanation without due reason, especially if one considers if the reasoning process itself met

74. Kuipers, "Naive and Refined Truth Approximation," 299.

75. Walton, *Informal Logic*, 212; Kahane, *Logic and Contemporary Rhetoric*, 79–81.

the criteria of evaluation mentioned in this and the next chapter. In the approach that I describe, if the explanation meets all the criteria of truth-testing, then the critic bears the burden of proof to demonstrate that such a relationship is fallacious. Abductive reasoning, being a defeasible argument, allows for future evidence to call into question the hypothesis. However, if the conclusion drawn is genuinely the best explanation, it will stand up to the scrutiny. One might argue that when there is "background information strongly opposed to such a causal connection, or the statistical sample in question is too small or unrepresentative, then we make a mistake in jumping to [a] conclusion that we've found a causal connection."[76] However, if that were the case, the hypothesis ought not to have been considered the best explanation in the first place. The criteria for evaluation should have led to a different conclusion. Therefore, if the abductive process led to a causal connection, it is more than reasonable to hold on to the explanation until further evidence proves otherwise.

Defense against Bas van Fraassen's Criticisms

Bas van Fraassen, Distinguished Professor of Philosophy at San Francisco State University, raises several objections to abductive reasoning, of which I will consider two. Although van Fraassen's criticisms deal specifically with abduction within the philosophy of science, his objections could cause issues with the abductive process as a whole, rendering it moot for any field of scholarship. Therefore, his criticisms deserve answers to consider abduction a viable philosophical tool.

Van Fraassen, at one point, argues that one could use abduction in scientific inquiry, but empirical adequacy and truth only connect when the theory considers that which is observable.[77] When one comes to a hypothesis from premises regarding the observable world, only then is the conclusion deemed empirically adequate and valid. If one draws a conclusion from unobservable premises (what he calls theoretical entities), then there is no way to connect with the truth, for anything unobservable is epistemically inaccessible.[78] This critique directly impacts Christian apologetics as numerous arguments base themselves on logical rules of inference (theoretical), not observed empirical data. Stathis Psillos adequately answers this

76. Kahane, *Logic and Contemporary Rhetoric*, 81.
77. van Fraassen, *The Scientific Image*, 71–72.
78. Psillos, "On Van Fraassen's Critique," 34.

objection, noting that it is presumptuous and wrong to assume that the epistemic status of beliefs based on observables is automatically superior to that of "unobservables."[79] It is biased to suppose that perception has a stronger foundation of justification than logical inferences. One should not hold unobservable data to some higher standard than observable data.

Van Fraassen's second criticism, related to the false alternatives fallacy, is often called the "argument from the bad lot." Van Fraassen argues that someone making the inference from the evidence must take a step beyond merely making a comparative judgment and must genuinely believe that they can find the true conclusion within hypotheses already available to them rather than any hypothesis that is not. However, the hypotheses readily available to the hypothesizer may all be rubbish. To claim to have the truth, the hypothesizer must assume that he possesses a privilege, a natural predisposition, for being able to determine the right range of hypotheses from which to choose.[80] So, for a Christian apologist to claim truth in his conclusions, he must claim that he possesses knowledge of all relevant hypotheses and can infer the best explanation from them. However, for van Fraassen, all the known relevant hypotheses might be entirely off. Thus, van Fraassen deems it necessary to exclude the possibility of the bad lot before giving warrant for calling a hypothesis empirically adequate and true.

As Psillos observes, this then leads to "bald scepticism" because "very few beliefs, if any, can be warranted if warrant involves elimination of the possibility that the belief may be false."[81] With the defeasibility of the abductive process, there is always a possibility that one could draw wrong conclusions, but to immediately assume that the truth lies outside known (or knowable) hypotheses is an error. One must consider that when discovering or choosing the best hypotheses, explanatory processes have played a role in guiding the process, so hypothesizers have taken caution in coming to their conclusions.[82] With a logical process in place and the possibility of generating a reasonable hypothesis (not merely choosing one out of a predetermined lot), van Fraassen's argument from the bad lot does not hinder the abductive process. Thus, his criticisms do not prevent abductive reasoning from being a tool for finding satisfactory and true conclusions in scientific, philosophical, or apologetic fields.

79. Psillos, "On Van Fraassen's Critique," 34–35.

80. van Fraassen, *Laws and Symmetry*, 142–43.

81. Psillos, "On Van Fraassen's Critique," 37.

82. Okasha, "Van Fraassen's Critique," 695.

Defense against Anthony Flew's Leaky Bucket Critique

One final criticism that attempts to undermine the abductive process specifically within Christian apologetic methodology is the "ten leaky buckets argument." Maintained by Antony Flew (who at the time was a staunch atheist), this argument states that if any solitary evidence, argument, or premise is weak and fails in itself to point to the truthfulness of a hypothesis, the accumulation of such proofs is unable to do any better in leading to a correct conclusion. He writes, "If one leaky bucket will not hold water that is not reason to think that ten can."[83] Alasdair MacIntyre makes a similar argument when he says, "One occasionally hears teachers of theology aver that although the proofs do not provide conclusive grounds for belief in God, they are at least pointers, indicators. But a fallacious argument points nowhere (except to the lack of logical acumen on the part of those who accept it). And three fallacious arguments are no better than one."[84]

From Flew's standpoint, a proof that has problems—has a leak in it and is unable to hold water—will not support an explanation even if it is joined together with nine other leaky buckets (arguments) that also support that explanation. Thus, an apologist may argue that although individual arguments such as the cosmological, teleological, and moral proofs each have problems and do not necessarily point with certainty to the Christian God, together, they form individual premises that support a cumulative case for the inference that God is the best explanation. Flew argues that since each argument has issues such that it separately cannot carry a burden of proof, cumulatively, a group of such arguments fares no better.

Paul Feinberg gives two strong answers to this criticism. First, Flew might have an argument if the proofs claim to substantiate a conclusion with certainty. However, that is not the case with abduction. Abductive reasoning leads to a hypothesis that is more probable than not given the accumulation of evidence that needs explanation and seems to point to the Christian worldview as the best explanation. The critic may come up with a different conclusion, but then the burden of proof shifts to the critic to demonstrate how their explanation is more plausible than the one the Christian apologist gave.[85] His second answer to the criticism is that the evidence and arguments used by the Christian apologist tend to reinforce one

---

83. Flew, *God & Philosophy*, 63.

84. MacIntyre, *Difficulties in Christian Belief*, 63.

85. Feinberg, "Cumulative Case Apologetics," 167.

another. Where one premise may be weak, a second premise strengthens it; thus, all the premises together are strong enough to support the conclusion. Feinberg answers Flew's metaphor, "Unless the holes in all ten buckets line up perfectly so that the water will spill out, one bucket may so reinforce another bucket so that the ten leaky buckets will indeed make a bucket that will carry water. The apologist is arguing that Christian theism is the best explanation of *all* available evidence *taken together*."[86] Thus, Flew's concern that accumulated weak premises do not support the hypothesis is itself an argument that has sprung a leak. Interestingly enough, Flew would later repudiate his atheism. He credits several arguments and pieces of evidence in science and mathematics that pointed to a creative intelligence as the origin of life. One could say that Flew no longer saw a leak in that bucket.[87]

While a type of logic that opens itself to defeaters, abduction still has many strengths that overcome perceived weaknesses. Abduction can choose or create hypotheses that best explain the data to high probabilities using a wide range of arguments and evidence. Even so, these criticisms highlight the necessity that if one is going to make truth claims about a given hypothesis/worldview, there need to be sound criteria to buttress the conclusion.

Criteria for Evaluating Worldview Hypotheses

Without careful analysis, one may overlook abductive reasoning as nothing more than mere guesswork. Some may argue that anyone could pick and choose whatever premises they wanted, which have no relation to one another, and then conclude with any off-the-wall explanation as proof for any presupposed theory they held (a charge often placed against the Christian worldview). Thus, it is necessary to consider if there are criteria for appraising the creation, choosing, or evaluation of a hypothesis/worldview which guide the process itself and lay the foundation for considering abduction a persuasive rational tool for philosophical thought.

Paul Feinberg notes that "to settle conflicting truth claims and determine what is the best explanation for all the data, there must be some tests for truth. The reason for this is simple: Christianity is not the only worldview that claims to be true."[88] While several hypotheses/worldviews claim to have abductively given the best explanation, there must be criteria

---

86. Feinberg, "Cumulative Case Apologetics," 167. Emphasis original.

87. Flew, *There Is a God*, 74–78.

88. Feinberg, "Cumulative Case Apologetics," 153.

to measure such contentions. Peirce considered that a hypothesis must possess three aspects if it is to be a likely explanation for the given evidence—this from a philosophy of science perspective. First, the hypothesis must have the ability to provide an account that explains all the facts under consideration. Second, the hypothesis must be testable; otherwise, it is nothing more than a mere suggestion until verified. Finally, it must be economical—a simple explanation.[89]

Christian theologians and apologists have put forth many different lists of criteria which help determine if a worldview is truthful and the best explanation. The lists are quite similar, so a composite should give an overall picture of what they suggest for hypothesis/worldview testing. First, the hypothesis must have explanatory viability—it must feasibly explain all the given premises. Next, the hypothesis must correspond with reality—it must agree with the facts and with the historical and empirical dimensions of existence. Then it must also have coherence—everything is conceptually linked without contradiction. Next, the hypothesis must be rational—there is a logical consistency in the causal explanation. Then it must be simple—it ought not need to contain multiple points to touch every fact. One prefers a simple hypothesis with a central point that explains the premises rather than something complicated. Also, it must be compatible with background theories—it cannot contradict theories it assumes are true. Finally, it must be able to accommodate counter-evidence, answering possible defeaters and criticisms others raise.

While helpful, such a long list may beg the question about the rationale for including these criteria. Without some form of reasoning for why a person includes this or that criterion, it may come across that the person just chose these benchmarks on a whim. Any included standards themselves ought to have some philosophical or logical support. The criteria for abductive hypothesis/worldview analysis that several worldview apologists use are tests of truth based upon the epistemological theories of truth (as explained in the next chapter). These criteria are neutral to all views, and therefore theorists cannot manipulate them to the advantage of a hypothesis they already hold. If a theistic hypothesis (i.e., Christian worldview) is the best inference, one cannot dismiss it offhand without further explanation.

89. Aliseda, *Abductive Reasoning*, 36.

Conclusion

Abductive reasoning has shown itself to be an expedient philosophical tool for use in apologetics and is worthy of further scholarly inquiry. As I have argued, abduction is particularly compelling in that it not only has strengths as a form of reasoning in itself and as a philosophical methodology, but it also more than adequately answers the criticisms against it. If one comes to the method knowing its limitations—that it does not prove certainty but can only lead one to the *probable* best explanation—one will not expect it to produce what it never was meant to produce. Some may argue that without certainty, it is weak. However, as Ronald Nash determines, "even though no worldview can rise above logical probability, it may still be believed with moral certainty. A single proposition or system of propositions that is only probable in the logical sense may still generate certainty in the psychological or moral sense."[90] It is not realistic to expect absolute certainty (from a rational, scientific, and philosophical standpoint) for such a task is impossible to attain for any human argument or evidence. This in no way denies the certainty of the truths espoused in Scripture. Instead, that which depends solely on human thinking and intellect cannot move much further than a substantial probability of truth as far as human understanding goes. Still, this probability can go a long way in arguing for the truthfulness of a worldview.

What abduction is meant to produce, it does so effectively. Given that numerous criteria are in place to ensure its credence as a methodology, it has the freedom and flexibility to utilize any available form or structure of evidence as its premises, and it can infer not only particular Christian doctrines but also the entire worldview, more than standing up to the criticisms raised against it. Abduction is an acceptable method for consideration in defense of the Christian faith. However, one needs to examine more closely the criteria proposed by several leading worldview apologists for using abduction to demonstrate how it tests the truthfulness of worldview hypotheses.

90. Nash, *Worldviews in Conflict*, 71.

4

Testing for the Truth, the Whole Truth, and Nothing but the Truth

" Truth is so obscure in these times, and falsehood so established,
that, unless we love the truth, we cannot know it."

—BLAISE PASCAL, *Pensées*

IN WHAT ONE CAN only describe as a shocking admission to the spirit of
the age, Oxford Dictionaries named "post-truth" as its "Word of the Year"
for AD 2016. Post-truth is "relating to or denoting circumstances in which
objective facts are less influential in shaping public opinion than appeals to
emotion and personal belief."[1] Such a blatant declaration reveals a movement in Western culture that steps away from a belief that there is an objective truth found in reality that everyone (who has reasoning capabilities)
ought to recognize and admit, in exchange for a creed of allowing one to
create truth and reality according to one's whim. Besides the obviously self-
defeating aspects of such beliefs (i.e., one cannot objectively claim any truth
to the statement that there is no objective truth), this also reveals that a
person's worldview manipulates their view of truth to a certain extent. Arlie
J. Hoover notes, "You can't possibly be a complete sceptic. A total sceptic

1. "Word of the Year 2016," *Oxford Dictionary*.

81

must say: 'There is no truth at all,' which is impossible to affirm because the proposition itself claims to be true. You'd be saying: 'It is a truth that there are no truths.' If there are no truths, then the proposition as a whole is false. The assertion destroys itself. A sceptic can't even affirm his scepticism without undercutting himself."[2] However, one would even need to test this aspect of a worldview for truthfulness. The lack of a fixed point of reference that is the truth of reality only causes confusion.

Abdu Murray likens the need for truth to a ride he took on a car ferry. While sitting in his car and looking at his radio, he did not see the ferry disembark from the shore nor feel it leave the dock. When he looked up, he saw the river moving but had that weird feeling of being unsure if he was moving or not. He notes that looking at the boat would not have helped because the boat also would have been moving, and the ever-flowing river provided no fixed point of reference. Only by looking at the land that never moved could he clear his confusion. The certainty of objective facts that truthfully reflect reality serves as such a reference point.[3] Whether people want to admit it or not, the truth is objective and absolute. "What is true is true for all people at all times in all places, whether they know it or not, believe it or not, and like it or not."[4]

Such an attack on truth might appear to place an apologist in a conundrum. If the apologist's worldview claims an objective truth, while the other person's worldview makes no such concession, can there ever be any meaningful dialogue, and is worldview analysis possible? Taking away the ability to find the truth is the death knell of any form of abstract reasoning or communication, for without it, language becomes meaningless. Without the existence of truth, there can be no exchange of ideas nor any meaningful discourse to come to an understanding of the universe. As Douglas Groothuis admits, "Without objective criteria, each worldview would be hermetically sealed off from other worldviews, since each would have its own truth claims and its own ways of verifying them. But if Christians desire to demonstrate the truth and rationality of Christianity to those who hold other worldviews, they must apply objective criteria to the contending worldviews. If none are given, there is no apologetic."[5]

2. Hoover, *Dear Agnos*, 23.

3. Murray, "Aspiring Angels."

4. Anderson, Clark, and Naugle, *Introduction to Christian Worldview*, 70.

5. Groothuis, *Christian Apologetics*, 51.

Thankfully, no matter how much the skeptics try, reality always has a way to continue on. A person may deny the truth all that they want, but in the end, the absolute truth of reality will always come to bear. Moreover, truth, by definition, has an exclusivity. If truth was all-inclusive, then nothing would be false. If nothing was false, then there would be no meaning to truth. Even still, armchair philosophers have muddied the waters about the concept itself. Vince Vitale says that there is confusion about the concept of truth, writing,

> We are very confused about the truth: There's the truth, and then there's the naked truth. There's the truth, and then there's the gospel truth (though the gospel is taken to be obviously false). There's the honest truth, and then there's the God's honest truth (but that has nothing to do with God). We stretch the truth and bend the truth and twist the truth. We bury the truth because the truth hurts. When we want something to be false, we knock on wood. When we want something to be true, we cross our fingers. Which wooden cross are we trusting in? Why do we have such a confused relationship with the truth? Fear. We're afraid of truth. Truth has so often been abused that experience has taught us the trajectory of truth—the trajectory of believing you are right and others are wrong—is from truth to disagreement to devaluing to intolerance to extremism to violence to terrorism. And if that is the trajectory, then those committed to truth are in fact terrorists in the making. If that is the trajectory, then truth is an act of war, and an act of war leaves you with only two options: fight or flee.[6]

Truth is a powerful weapon indeed.

In the Bible, Pilate asked Jesus, "What is truth?" but then walked away without receiving the answer (John 18:38). Philosophers have argued that question for many millennia, and there was agreement (until recently) that there is such a thing as objective truth, and any claim of truth is testable. To communicate truth is to give words that represent objective reality as it actually exists. To make truth subjective is to manipulate it to one's own fancy. Since truth is real and objective, truth has specific attributes. "When we use the word truth, truth by its nature is non-contradictory. It doesn't violate the basic laws of logic. Truth is absolute—it does not depend on time, place or conditions. . . . Truth is discovered. It exists independently of our minds. . . . Truth is descriptive—it is the agreement of the mind with reality. . . . Truth is inescapable—to deny truth's existence is to affirm it. . . .

6. Vitale, "The Trajectory of Truth."

Truth is unchanging—it is the firm standard by which truth claims can be measured. There has to be something eternal, beyond time, culture, and relativities of human existence. It is the standard by which we can judge."[7]

Based on this high view of truth, people need to rightly and objectively analyze their worldview and the worldview of others for truth. Without such a high view of the truth, a person is vulnerable to the manipulation of those who would attempt to shape truth to their own nefarious ends, and that person is unable to enjoy the freedom and fulfillment of life that the truth makes available to the individual.[8] A worldview (even one that denies such a thing as truth) makes truth claims. It is at this point where one compares worldviews for apologetic purposes—do the claims of a worldview sync with truth?

To answer that question and to compare the claims between worldviews, there must be criteria to test for worldview truthfulness.[9] A worldview is only as good as its relationship to truth; therefore, every worldview is open to scrutiny. Worldviews as systematic belief structures make claims about truth and assertions about reality—so they are only meaningful insofar as they give a narrative about objective truths.[10] Those narratives are thus comparable at the points of their truth claims. William P. Alston says, "*Everything* we believe can be assessed for truth value. Therefore our interpretation of truth affects the status of everything we believe, whatever the subject matter. And if our concept of truth is a realist one, then *all* our beliefs owe their truth value to the fact that they are related in a certain way to a reality beyond themselves."[11] That means one can weigh the entirety of the belief structure of a worldview against reality. Just because a worldview makes such truth claims does not mean that it answers every possible question about reality and human existence, nor that it is without gaps. However, the question then becomes whether or not a worldview fits reality and can fill in the gaps consistently. "Because various worldviews come to fundamentally different conclusions about the big questions of life, logic and reason mandate that not all perspectives can be true. The rational choice of one particular position ought to be made—and can be made—via testing and evaluation."[12]

7. McAllister, "Truth and Reality."

8. Guinness, *Time for Truth*, 82–85.

9. Hoover, *Dear Agnos*, 26.

10. Groothuis, *Christian Apologetics*, 76.

11. Alston, *Realist Conception of Truth*, 8. Emphasis original.

12. Samples, *A World of Difference*, 28.

However, worldview claims are verifiable for truth only to the point that those claims are capable of corroboration by objective truth-tests that lie outside the worldview itself (as much as possible). The exact criteria for determining if something is true has been the debate of philosophers for many centuries. As mentioned in the previous chapter, any criteria chosen ought to have some sort of basis. Therefore, it is crucial that truth-tests are acceptable and applicable for all people regardless of their worldview—a standard that appeals to humanity's sense of reasoning to see the difference between truth and error among the varied worldviews.[13] While most worldview apologists had recognized two underlying theories of truth (correspondence and coherence), I believe that with the added pragmatic theory of truth these theories give apologists three epistemological principles of truth that then undergird three truth-tests for worldviews.[14] Taken together, these three tests demonstrate the truthfulness or falseness of a belief structure by revealing whether the worldview holds up to the scrutiny of the data revealed by the tests.

Epistemological Theories of Truth

Philosophers have both upheld and criticized all three epistemological theories through rigorous debate. I contend that while all three have both strengths and weaknesses, the three placed together make a stronger case for truth than any single theory on its own. That is, if the points of belief in a worldview meet the scrutiny of all three theories (as filtered through the abductive reasoning process), then that worldview has strong evidence to claim truth for itself. Moreover, these three theories of truth undergird the means for abductively testing worldview truthfulness or falsity. This chapter first considers what the three epistemological theories of truth state and their strengths and weaknesses. Then, it considers the three tests for truth that they generate for worldview analysis.

Coherence Theory

A coherence theory of truth argues that when a belief coheres to the other beliefs within one's noetic (rational) structure (or, for the purposes of this

---

13. Story, *Christianity on the Offense*, 41–42.

14. See Anderson, Clark, and Naugle, *An Introduction to Christian Worldview*, 70–90.

book, if a belief coheres with other beliefs within one's worldview—the belief structure), then it is more likely that belief is true. If the premises of a person's belief structure offer no contradiction to one another or the known laws of logic, then it is more likely that the whole structure is true. If something does not fit within a system of what is known to be true or what has happened in one's experience, it is rejected as false.[15] Donald G. Bloesch writes that, according to this theory, "The meaning of the part can only be understood through the meaning of the whole. The measure of truth is the illumination and integration of our total experience in the light of an overarching idea or principle. A proposition is said to be true if it fits into an all-encompassing logical system."[16] He highlights that a solitary belief is only as good as the worldview of which it is a part. Still, if there is a single belief within an entire structure that is false, this demonstrates a fault within the structure itself—the worldview as a whole has less probability of truth when individual beliefs within it do not sync with one another or with the known laws of logic. It is possible to recognize coherence in a belief system because the universe itself is a coherent system—a belief or proposition is true because it "fits into the one comprehensive account of the universe or reality."[17]

Within coherence, there are no varying levels of beliefs that would justify the inclusion of false beliefs that are not fundamental to the overall structure (i.e., a form of foundationalism that would allow for false non-basic beliefs as long as the basic beliefs are still intact). J. P. Moreland and William Lane Craig explain this theory, "The essence of coherentism lies in the fact that there are no asymmetries between basic and nonbasic beliefs. All beliefs are on a par with each other, and the main, or more likely, sole source of the justification of a beliefs is the fact that the belief appropriately 'coheres' with the other beliefs in one's noetic structure. . . . The coherence theories of truth [mean], roughly, the notion that a proposition is true if and only if it is part of a coherent set of propositions."[18] What sets coherence apart from other theories is that "truth does not consist in the holding of some correspondence between the proposition and some reality which obtains independent of anything that may be believed about it."[19] The em-

---

15. Cotham, *One World, Many Neighbors*, 44.
16. Bloesch, *The Ground of Certainty*, 130.
17. White, *Truth*, 110.
18. Moreland and Craig, *Philosophical Foundations*, 109–10.
19. Walker, "The Coherence Theory," 124.

phasis, then, is if a particular claim or belief is consistent with a specific set or structure of beliefs (for my purposes, a worldview).

It would seem (in a knee-jerk reaction to the theory) that mere coherence is not enough on several grounds. One might argue that one could have several consistent beliefs that may be true in and of themselves, yet they have no positive connection between them. But Dan O'Brien recognizes that the coherence theory necessitates that there must be a relationship between beliefs, stating, "A coherent belief system is therefore one that lacks logical contradiction, one that is not probabilistically inconsistent, and one in which there are inferential relations between its constituent beliefs."[20] Random propositions do not make a coherent belief system—for it to be a system, there must be relations between the beliefs and propositions that constitute the position.

Another possible problem with this theory is that it initially appears that it does nothing to distinguish between truth and falsity—premises may cohere, but that does not make them true. Therefore, there would appear to be a need for one to obtain the beliefs independently from one another. This critique may open the theory to criticisms of advocating a relativity of truth—if one's particular set of beliefs all cohere, then it is true regardless of what is really the case or whether or not it correctly represents the world. It may also open the theory to the criticism that beliefs create the truth rather than the other way around. Coherence theorists would deny this—it is not if a belief coheres with the rest of one's beliefs at a particular moment, but if a belief coheres to the specific beliefs that determine the truth.[21] Of course, as Ralph Walker himself admits, a pure coherence theory is untenable, so an impure coherence theory that recognizes that there are at least some propositions for which truth consists in correspondence may be stronger (although he also confessed that this does not make the problems with the correspondence theory disappear).[22]

Regardless of the strengths or weaknesses of coherence, this theory is vital in that it demonstrates why pluralism cannot work. If two worldviews hold contradictory statements from one another, they do not cohere; therefore, both cannot be true. It is also important in that the theory demonstrates a flaw in a worldview system if there are contradictory beliefs within the system itself or if there are contradictions of worldview beliefs with the

---

20. O'Brien, *Introduction to the Theory of Knowledge*, sect. 2, chap. 7.

21. Walker, "The Coherence Theory," 135.

22. Walker, "The Coherence Theory," 154.

fundamental laws of logic. Moreover, any time a false system attempts to integrate the truth into its system, it will find that it refutes itself somehow. J. Mark Bertrand indicates this problem when he writes,

> Any time an unbelieving worldview borrows truth, a problem of coherence will develop: the truth doesn't fit within a network of lies. As fallen creatures, we are perfectly capable of holding contradicting ideas in tension (in fact, we can even hold them in the mistaken belief that they are not in tension). But when the contradictions are pointed out to us, we question the validity of the system. Even people who revel in paradox and despise logic don't like to be accused of holding contradictory positions unknowingly. Once a person begins to doubt the fundamental coherence of his perspective, he will test it in terms of observed reality. Are there better solutions to the problems around me? If his own beliefs (from which he is already in the process of distancing himself) do not produce solutions, perhaps other, more coherent beliefs would. This is the mind-set the worldview apologist aims to provoke.[23]

Thus, coherence has its place since a worldview that lacks coherence has a high probability of being false. That being the case, logical consistency is a specific test for truth birthed from this theory.

Bertrand further indicates that coherence is not enough to find the solution to the truth problem, but one must find beliefs that correspond with reality for them to be true. Donald Davidson denotes that "a coherence theory seems at a loss to provide any reason for a believer to believe that his beliefs, if coherent, are true"; he, therefore, believes that, to accept the coherence theory of truth, it must be consistent with correspondence and must allow for a "nonrelativized, noninternal form of realism."[24] Kenneth Samples agrees as he states, "Coherence is a necessary condition for truth but not a sufficient one. In other words, truth must contain coherence, but coherence isn't all that is needed in order to possess truth. . . . Incoherence shows that a worldview must be false; coherence shows that a worldview may be true. As important as coherence is, more is needed for a worldview to pass the ultimate truth test."[25] Arlie J. Hoover also agrees in that he does not believe it was possible to have a complete worldview by coherence since one can

23. Bertrand, *Rethinking Worldview*, 201.
24. Davidson, "Coherence Theory of Truth," 139–40, 146.
25. Samples, *A World of Difference*, 33.

"build an elaborate system of propositions that are all coherent but false;" instead, "coherence must forever remain wedded to correspondence."[26]

Correspondence Theory

The correspondence theory of truth states that for a belief or other form of proposition to be true, it must correspond to reality; that is, whatever the proposition represents actually exists as fact.[27] To deem something as true is independent of the one holding onto the belief. As William P. Alston explains, "A statement (proposition, belief . . .) is true if and only if what the statement says to be the case actually is the case. . . . There are no epistemic requirements for the truth of my statement. . . . So long as [for example, if I stated that gold is malleable, and that is the case], then what I said is true, whatever the epistemic status of that proposition for any individual or community."[28] Therefore, truth is not only a matter of what one holds in their mind or intellect but also a question of whether what is held in the mind accurately reflects what actually exists.[29] Some view an independent reality as problematic—would a fact be true if there was no one to think or verbalize it as such? This surely would be the case since the thought or statement merely reflects reality.

For there to be communication and discussion about truth, one expresses beliefs and propositions verbally or in writing through language. It is important to note that one considers the expression of belief (as far as it is commonly understood) true or false as long as the basic elements of the expression accurately reflect reality—that is, as the words or expressions and the world correspond to one another. For Ludwig Wittgenstein (in his earlier works), a proposition is true as long as it is in complete agreement with its smallest fact-stating unit, the truth-possibilities of what he calls elementary propositions.[30] Later in his writings, Wittgenstein would distance himself from such possibilities since it is seemingly impossible to interact with a fact itself without dependence on human judgment. While this exposes some weaknesses in the correspondence theory of truth, this

26. Hoover, *Dear Agnos*, 47.

27. Moreland and Craig, *Philosophical Foundations*, 118.

28. Alston, *Realist Conception of Truth*, 5–6.

29. Thomas Aquinas, *Summa Theologica*, 1 Q 16 a.1.

30. Wittgenstein, *Tractatus Logico-Philosophicus*, 4.4; see also Thiselton, "Truth," 894–95.

in no way eliminates the possibility of expressing beliefs in such a way that they reflect what truly is. As W. V. Quine explains the theory, "The truth predicate is an intermediary between words and the world. What is true is the sentence [belief, proposition], but its truth consists in the world's being as the sentence [belief, proposition] says."[31] So, a belief or other form of a proposition is true only if it reflects the state of affairs of the world—it exists outside the individual as reflected by the described statement, and one consciously experiences it as such.[32]

This theory is important in analyzing worldviews, for "a good worldview will have a strong foundation in correspondence; it will have factual support. Furthermore, it will include all kinds of data. . . . A good worldview will seek to integrate all kinds of data into a meaningful, coherent picture."[33] The beliefs that make up the structure of the worldview must accurately reflect what truly exists within the world. Abduction fits nicely here, gathering the facts against which one may test a worldview. Worldview apologetics weighs all the data since there is "no single argument that is guaranteed to persuade every unbeliever or to assuage every doubt in a believer's heart. But since every fact testifies to . . . reality . . . the apologist has no shortage of resources, but rather a great abundance."[34] Therefore, important parts of a worldview's belief structure must be available for empirical scrutiny, although other parts may be more abstract and logical and therefore open for analysis of its evidential consistency.

Since not every aspect of a worldview is measurable or available for analysis from the scope of a correspondence theory of truth, hanging the entirety of one's grounds for truthfulness upon this one theory is not tenable. As Hoover indicates, "A far greater limitation to the Correspondence Theory is the simple fact that there is much of reality with which we can't directly 'correspond.' You simply can't 'check the referent' every time you wish. Much, maybe most, of reality outruns our direct investigative powers. Not being omniscient, we must close the knowledge gap with another method of truth-finding. Enter the Coherence Theory! If we can't correspond with all reality, the only way we can ever escape the tyranny of

31. Quine, *Pursuit of Truth*, 81.

32. Hoover, *Dear Agnos*, 45–46.

33. Hoover, *Dear Agnos*,49.

34. Frame, *Apologetics to the Glory of God*, 64.

the immediate and have a worldview—a view of the entire universe—is to round out the Correspondence Theory with the Coherence Theory."[35]

So, one needs the correspondence theory of truth for an overall analysis of the truthfulness of the system, but it is not enough. One must couple it with the coherence theory of truth, where each is brought closer to analyzing whether a singular belief or an entire belief system of a worldview reflects the truth. Therefore, the beliefs that make up a worldview must both correspond to reality and cohere with one another logically. To lose either of these demonstrates the system as most probably false. However, one more epistemological theory of truth undergirds the truth-testing process of worldviews—the pragmatic theory of truth.

Pragmatic Theory

The pragmatic theory of truth requires something to be livable and useful. One experiences an idea or belief as true as it bears practical fruit in a subject's life. As William James, one of its earliest proponents, explains, "*True ideas are those that we can assimilate, validate, corroborate and verify. False ideas are those that we can not. . . .* The truth of an idea is not a stagnant property inherent in it. Truth *happens* to an idea. It *becomes* true, is *made* true by events. Its verity *is* in fact an event, a process: the process namely of its verifying itself, its veri-*fication* [sic]. Its validity is the process of its valid-*ation* [sic]."[36] So the epistemological status of a belief is not merely a stagnant mental exercise of data comparison or deep logical analysis but is very active—truth is truth when it works. As James further explains, "You can say of it then either that 'it is useful because it is true' or that 'it is true because it is useful.' Both these phrases mean exactly the same thing, namely that here is an idea that gets fulfilled and can be verified. True is the name for whatever idea starts the verification-process, useful is the name for its completed function in experience. True ideas would never have been singled out as such, would never have acquired a class-name, least of all a name suggesting value, unless they had been useful from the outset in this way."[37]

The truth of an idea is only verifiable as it leads to a worthwhile practical experience since, according to the pragmatic theory, truth is truth only when connected to livability. James further states, "Primarily, and on the

35. Hoover, *Dear Agnos*, 46.

36. James, *Pragmatism*, 201. Emphasis original.

37. James, *Pragmatism*, 204.

common-sense level, the truth of a state of mind means this function of *a leading that is worth while*. When a moment in our experience, of any kind whatever, inspires us with a thought that is true, that means that sooner or later we dip by that thought's guidance into the particulars of experience again and make advantageous connexion with them."[38] James' fellow pragmatist John Dewey explains, "*If* ideas, meanings, conceptions, notions, theories, systems are instrumental to an active reorganization of the given environment, to a removal of some specific trouble and perplexity, then the test of their validity and value lies in accomplishing this work. If they succeed in their office, they are reliable, sound, valid, good, true. If they fail to clear up confusion, to eliminate defects, if they increase confusion, uncertainty and evil when they are acted upon, then are they false."[39] Thus, truth is grounded in experience within the context of concrete social and behavioral settings, and one discovers truth through complete human involvement, not merely cold, detached observation from afar.[40] So a belief (or another form of proposition) represents reality not only when it explains experience soundly but also when it is fruitful in dealing with the practicality of life laid before it—not merely giving an abstract or theoretical explanation.[41]

C. I. Lewis espoused a further consideration with his conceptual pragmatism. As one experiences the world, one holds certain concepts and principles that interpret what one encounters—the a priori. Thus, the concepts and words that one uses to express the experience have pragmatic value. The truth or falsity of one's conceptual scheme (chosen for pragmatic reasons) determines how one experiences and interprets what occurs and what words one uses to explain them.[42] Thus, not only are the experiences themselves of truth value, but the concepts that interpret them and the words that explain them are also essential parts of one's understanding of truth.

This theory, like the others, is not without its problems. Moreland and Craig note, "Advocates of pragmatism claim that problems with the other two theories, our inability to transcend our theories (language, beliefs) and get to the external world (if there is such a thing; most pragmatists are antirealists) all favor pragmatism. Critics claim that it is self-refuting, that in their defense of the view, its advocates do not recommend pragmatism

38. James, *Pragmatism* 205. Emphasis original.

39. Dewey, *Reconstruction in Philosophy*, 156. Emphasis original.

40. Bloesch, *The Ground of Certainty*, 133.

41. Thiselton, "Truth," 896.

42. Lewis, *Mind and the World-Order*, 31–38.

because the theory is itself 'useful' but because it corresponds to certain facts about language, scientific theory testing and so forth, that it is a form of relativism, and that it fails the phenomenological argument for the correspondence theory."[43] Critics also claim that "a false belief may help someone to come to terms with life, or may help him to see the way forward in a particular situation; but this does not make it true."[44] In reality, determining causal connections between a belief and its benefits is difficult enough, much less to claim truthfulness. Someone may argue that the sight of a squirrel in a tree caused them to reconsider life choices such that they quit smoking, but to be able to say that such a thing is true is difficult without some corroboration of it also corresponding to reality and cohering to the rest of a person's belief system.

However, the pragmatic theory of truth raises an important consideration regarding worldview analysis. Part of the truthfulness of a worldview is that it is livable. It is one thing to hold onto a worldview hypothesis as a theory for existence, but it is another to live out that worldview in real life faithfully. A worldview can make many lofty claims that look good on paper or sound intelligent in an academic discussion, but if it places itself beyond the ability of its adherents to live out, then the 'theory' loses its truthfulness no matter how much empirical verification it claims to have or how logically consistent it might at first seem.

By no means are these three the only theories of truth propounded by philosophers, yet they have some of the deepest roots in the discussion of truth. While the three have their strengths and weaknesses, one finds that together they undergird one another enough that if a worldview can meet all three theories, it has a higher probability of being true than any other worldview. These three theories of truth bear three tests of truth by which inquirers scrutinize worldviews.

Tests for Truth in Worldview Analysis

These three epistemological theories of truth then undergird three tests (or criteria) to measure the truthfulness of not only the individual beliefs of a worldview but also the entire system itself. The question is if worldview A meets the tests of truth and satisfies the criteria better than worldview B.[45]

43. Moreland and Craig, *Philosophical Foundations*, 132.

44. Thiselton, "Truth," 897.

45. Wainwright, *Philosophy of Religion*, 173.

It is not enough for a worldview to meet only one of these tests. A worldview might have beliefs that correspond with reality but are not coherent with one another. Alternatively, a worldview may have coherence, but the system is not livable or pragmatic. Therefore, it is crucial to have a series of tests that match the varied ways humanity interacts with reality.

Graham Cole recognizes,

> Our [worldview] matters. We all have at least one, or maybe bits of different ones that we have never been able to connect up into some sort of coherent whole. Perhaps this is a question to which we have not really turned our minds in a sustained way. If we do then the real question becomes: So where do we find a frame of reference or a worldview that tells a coherent and consistent story that really understands us and illuminates the actual world in which we live? We need—if we want to be thoughtful about it—a frame of reference that is thinkable, that is, one that is not riddled with self-contradiction. It also needs to be livable—that is, we can actually live as though this frame of reference really does correspond to the world of our experience, so that we do not have to pretend that it does.[46]

McAllister also recognizes these three tests as the means of scrutinizing worldviews, stating, "Any worldview that would say it gives answers to reality and truth must do certain things.... First, it must be logically consistent. There must be a worldview that does not contradict itself.... Secondly, is it factual? Does it actually fit the facts of life? Does it help us to live life? Does it explain life adequately? Can we do things as a result of that.... The third thing is its viability—its ability to be lived out in the real world."[47] J. Mark Bertrand likens living out a worldview to following a map. For someone to ensure that the map they follow is accurate and will lead them to the correct destination, there are questions they might ask of the map itself before following its directions. Likewise, "You can test a worldview the same way you would test a map, by asking yourself if it matches reality, if the proportions are right, and if it gets you to the right destination. In more formal terms, we would call these tests correspondence, coherence, and productivity."[48]

Thus, scholarship has recognized that for a worldview to be true, it must pass all three tests. The coherence theory of truth begets the test

---

46. Cole, *Do Christians Have a Worldview?*, 4.

47. McAllister, "Truth and Reality."

48. Bertrand, *Rethinking Worldview*, 33.

of logical consistency—does the worldview have an internal consistency amongst its varied beliefs, and does it follow the known laws of logic? The correspondence theory of truth begets the test of empirical adequacy— although some beliefs may be of the supernatural kind that one cannot necessarily inspect through empirical verification, is there a broad scope of beliefs within the worldview that explains the world as it is (i.e., corresponds with reality)? Finally, the pragmatic theory of truth begets the test of experiential relevance—does the worldview have practical application to living in the world (i.e., can one live out the claims of the worldview)? Like the epistemological theories of truth, on their own, the tests do not adequately demonstrate the truthfulness or falseness of a worldview, but together they give the best chance of coming to accurate conclusions.

Logical Consistency

It is a fact that "truth will always be wholly consistent within itself, displaying internal logical harmony. [The logical consistency] test stresses the crucial unity and relatedness of all truth. Therefore any logical inconsistency in the basic elements of a worldview is a mark of essential error."[49] This test asks if the worldview is rational and makes sense. Since truth will always be entirely consistent with itself, harmonizing in every possible way, so too a worldview that has beliefs that reflect truth will display internal logical coherence.[50] One can consider this from succeeding angles. First, a logically consistent worldview conforms to the three fundamental laws of logic (the law of identity, the law of the excluded middle, and the law of non-contradiction).[51] Thus, the beliefs of a worldview will consistently conform to these deductive laws of logic. Ensuring logical consistency does not mean that a worldview will have no paradoxes (seemingly self-contradictory or absurd statements that, upon further inspection, are found not to contradict but rather merely confound). As Geisler and Watkins warn, "We can eliminate a world view if it has actual contradictions in any of its essential premises. However, we must be sure that the contradictions are real and not merely apparent. We must be dealing with real antinomies, not merely mysteries. A real contradiction occurs when two truth claims are given and one is the logical opposite of the other (they are logically

49. Samples, *A World of Difference*, 33.
50. Samples, *A World of Difference*, 33.
51. Moreland and Craig, *Philosophical Foundations*, 120.

contradictory, not merely contrary)."[52] Thus, this test measures if a worldview's essential beliefs remain consistent with the known laws of logic without true contradiction.

Thus, stemming from the laws of logic, a truthful worldview will not have any essential beliefs that contradict one another. Here, one tests whether a belief or proposition contained within a worldview "coheres with, that is, is logically deducible from, some of the other propositions, and ultimately the axioms, of its system. It is characteristic of the parts of a logical system . . . that no part would be what it is if its logical relations to the other parts were different from what they are."[53] It is necessary to demonstrate logical consistency since "any system of belief that is internally inconsistent is false."[54] Hoover explains, "A good worldview should have a high degree of coherence or internal consistency. One of the quickest ways to kill a system is to show self-contradiction. . . . It's like being killed with a hatpin stuck through the heart; the wound is tiny but death is just as certain. If, for example, your system affirms both determinism and free will you have a problem; you'll need some fancy footwork to show how both can be true at the same time."[55]

However, as I argued earlier, having an apologetic reach perfect certainty rather than a high degree of probability is nearly impossible. One also notices a difficulty for someone to thoroughly explain or map out a perfect consistency within their belief system. As Hoover clarifies, "I say a good worldview should have 'a high degree of consistency'—why not say 'perfect consistency?' I'm not sure any mortal could ever achieve perfect consistency, especially in dealing with the whole universe!"[56] It might be difficult to expect someone to explain every logical connection in their belief system. Nevertheless, showing that the major beliefs and claims of a worldview either remain consistent or contradict one another is an achievable goal for this test.

A necessary caveat in this discussion is that the essential, fundamental elements of a worldview must accord with one another—those beliefs and propositions that are necessary for the worldview itself (e.g., the resurrection of Jesus in Christianity). Any inconsistencies between these beliefs

52. Geisler and Watkins, *Worlds Apart*, 263.

53. White, *Truth*, 111.

54. Feinberg, "Cumulative Case Apologetics," 154.

55. Hoover, *Dear Agnos*, 48–49.

56. Hoover, *Dear Agnos*, 49.

(whether one would consider them basic or not) are fatal to the worldview's veracity. However, there may be smaller, secondary issues of doctrine or dogma within a worldview where differences or inconsistencies between various adherents do no damage to the worldview itself (i.e., the beliefs are not necessary for the worldview to answer life's most fundamental questions). An example is the debate among different Christian denominations over the mode of baptism—sprinkling of infants or immersion of those who profess faith. While an important matter of faith, it is not a core belief of the worldview itself; therefore, these inconsistencies do not invalidate the whole system. The testing of worldview should take place while analyzing its core, best-represented forms and not by eccentricities added by its followers.[57] Geisler and Watkins explain, "The actual contradiction must be between essential premises of a world view. If either or both of the contradictory premises are nonessential, the contradiction does not necessarily falsify the world view. All one needs to do is discard the nonessential premises which occasioned the contradiction. Throwing away the nonessential will not affect the essential view."[58]

It is worth noting that, although all the fundamental laws of logic are at play in this test, the lynchpin is the law of non-contradiction (sometimes referred to as the law of contradiction). This law states that two antithetical statements or propositions cannot be true simultaneously under the same conditions.[59] "The principle of non-contradiction needs to be observed. 'A' cannot be non-'A' at both the same time and in the same respect. A typewriter cannot be blue all over and red all over at the same time and in the same respect."[60] The law of non-contradiction is not some Western contraption brought about by Aristotle, nor is it merely philosophical wordplay. Everyday experience bears witness—it is either one truth or its opposite, but not both. The law of non-contradiction is inescapable because the moment someone refutes it, they actually uphold it. This inescapable law is why pluralism as a phenomenon is invalid. When the beliefs of one worldview directly contradict the beliefs of another worldview, combining them does not somehow wash this away.

A worldview that contradicts itself or the laws of logic is false, and one may declare it as such if it fails this test. However, it is not enough to say that

57. Groothuis, *Christian Apologetics*, 53–54.

58. Geisler and Watkins, *Worlds Apart*, 263.

59. Cotham, *One World, Many Neighbors*, 46.

60. Cole, "Do Christians Have a Worldview?," 22.

it is true merely because a worldview is consistent. A worldview may have consistent propositions of beliefs, but they do not correspond with reality. Thus, it is necessary to place worldviews under further scrutiny.

Empirical Adequacy

The second test for worldview truthfulness, based upon the correspondence theory of truth, is empirical adequacy, where there are inspections and verification of correspondence between worldview beliefs and a referent in the real world. It examines if there is a way to verify the facts of stated beliefs in a worldview—is there support for the claims a worldview expounds? This test asks questions of the worldview, such as: "Does the worldview fit with reality, and is it capable of offering cogent explanations or interpretations of the totality of things? Does the worldview adequately cover and explain all the data? Is the worldview, to put it in slightly different terms, true to the way things are? Does it cover the whole of life in an adequate way?"[61] David Naugle further explains, "If large chunks of human experience are neglected or negated by the worldview, if it seems incapable of opening up and elucidating important domains of the human experience and the cosmos, then the worldview, or aspects of it, is rendered suspect. A cogent *Weltanschauung* ought to be empirically comprehensive in its coverage and strong in its explanations."[62]

Not every single belief needs to have an equivalent empirical referent. There may be certain spiritual beliefs regarding heaven or paradise, or possibly spiritual agents, which delve into unseen realms that one cannot measure (although these beliefs must then be consistent with beliefs about the visible world). However, a reasonable worldview will not lack a connection between its beliefs and the real world—one has the capacity of investigating, evaluating, and critiquing a worldview's central claims and find that the beliefs have factual support (be they historical, scientific, or otherwise).[63] That is, enough of the claims of a worldview are available for some form of empirical testing and verifiable for correspondence with what actually exists. Then, the "greater the extent to which a worldview's essential factual claims can be established in various empirical, scientific and

---

61. Naugle, *Worldview*, 327.

62. Naugle, *Worldview*, 327. Emphasis original.

63. Samples, *A World of Difference*, 35.

historical ways, the greater is the likelihood that this worldview is true."[64] On the other hand, if worldview claims conflict with what is generally known to be true about reality (such as holding a belief in a flat earth which science of all forms regards as wrong), it is right to point out these divergences.[65]

Testing for empirical adequacy does not mean that every worldview interprets all empirical pieces of information similarly. However, a worldview is questionable if it "ignores or is inconsistent with human experience."[66] This test also does not mean that the worldview must give an account for every historical or scientific fact that exists. Instead, "the facts of history and science must be understandable in context of the worldview. . . . A worldview consistent with external reality will not fly in the face of what people universally experience and intuitively recognize as reality."[67] Of course, one must be careful not to make history, general sciences, and social sciences the end-all-be-all. Beliefs about scientific theories and historical events have changed in light of new evidence. Still, that which has been generally accepted and generally experienced can serve as a guide for testing a worldview. Thus, one can accept a worldview as reflecting truth when shown to be in harmony with and corroborated by the facts of science and history.[68]

However, just because a worldview has one belief with an empirical basis does not automatically make it true. Instead, when the accumulation of a worldview's beliefs corresponds with reality, the more likely that worldview is true. James Orr argues, "It is not one line of evidence only which establishes [a] position, but the concurrent force of many, starting from different and independent standpoints."[69] Thus, a worldview should have several lines of empirical evidence. As strong as this accumulation of evidence might be, it still is not enough to claim truth for a worldview (although a lack of empirical adequacy does illuminate the falseness of a worldview). Apologists perform this test on worldviews in conjunction with the other two tests, including the third of experiential relevance.

---

64. Groothuis, *Christian Apologetics*, 55.

65. Nash, *Worldviews in Conflict*, 57.

66. Nash, *Worldviews in Conflict*, 58–59.

67. Story, *Christianity on the Offense*, 48.

68. Orr, *Christian View of God*, 87.

69. Orr, *Christian View of God*, 111.

Experiential Relevance

Based on the pragmatic theory of truth, this test analyzes a worldview for its livability—a worldview must not only seem theoretically sound but must be experientially relevant in the life of its adherent.[70] This test asks the worldview if it has significance for human experience with meaningful applications for a person's life, including how it deals with such vital areas as ethics, suffering, death, and human meaning. Moreover, on a more personal level, it asks how the worldview meets the individual's daily life. A worldview must not only be intellectually satisfying but also harmonize with lived experience and behavior.[71] If someone claims a particular worldview but cannot live out its natural consequences, this gives reason to question whether the worldview is adequate for someone to embrace as a means of living truly. As an example of how an unlivable worldview exposes itself, Graham Cole relates the following, "Bertrand Russell tells the story of a woman who had discovered a philosophical view known as solipsism. Solipsism maintains that the only consciousness to be found is your own. She wrote to Russell wondering why more people weren't solipsists. In other words, she didn't live as though solipsism were true to fact (i.e., the actual state of affairs)."[72]

Os Guinness notes, "Again and again the lesson is simple: all thoughts can be thought, but not all thoughts can be lived. So we should never stop halfway with skepticism [or other worldviews], but insist on pressing ideas uncompromisingly to their conclusion"[73] He rightly argues that beliefs have consequences. To hold to a particular belief means that a certain lifestyle or life-choice is the natural result. However, if that natural result is not livable or is not relevant to the existential existence of a person, then one must rethink their worldview position. Guinness continues, "At some point the falseness [of a worldview] shows through [at the point of experiential relevance], and at that moment they will experience extreme cognitive dissonance, so that it is no longer in their best interest to continue to persist in believing what they believed until then. When they reach this point, they are facing up to their dilemma, and they will be open to rethinking their

70. Feinberg, "Cumulative Case Apologetics," 155.

71. Sire, *Naming the Elephant*, 117.

72. Cole, "Do Christians Have a Worldview?", 31.

73. Guinness, "Turning the Tables."

position in a profound way."[74] This apologetic approach tries to bring the bearer of a false worldview to the point of questioning their worldview and seeing the glories of the Christian worldview.

Guinness relates a story that demonstrates this point. After giving a lecture at a university in northern England, a non-Christian professor approached him, saying that Guinness challenged him through what he shared. Having been known for resistance to the Christian faith, the man found an unusual dissonance between his own beliefs and its resultant lifestyle with what he then wanted for his newborn daughter. He and his wife lived out an open marriage, but they did not want that lifestyle for their daughter. Faced with the dilemma of the consequences of their worldview (a worldview that they could not even allow for their daughter), they had to find a worldview that was livable in what they realized was the only way to live.[75]

However, within this test, Guinness gives some wise warnings. First, apologists should never confuse a person's worldview with the person himself. A false worldview takes away no value from the person as a person. Second, no person will ever live out their worldview perfectly. Every individual seems to live their worldview in their own way. Finding a perfect example of a lived-out worldview is rare—there are no textbook versions.[76] That said, the beliefs within a worldview are open to the criticism of experiential relevancy. Any worldview that does not touch upon the critical issues of life that every person deals with, or whose beliefs are practically unlivable, are suspect, and one ought to call them to task. However, a worldview that gives answers to the essential areas of life and gives a livable way of life is open for serious consideration.

Again, this solitary test is not enough to determine the truth or falsity of a system but is an essential component in tangent with the others. A worldview might appear livable, but if it is not logically consistent with the known laws of logic, or has incoherence within itself, or has no empirical adequacy, then it has a higher probability of being false. Just as the three theories of truth in themselves are not necessarily enough to explain truth, the three tests by themselves individually are not enough to demonstrate worldview truthfulness. Yet, when taken together, the three tests are reliable

74. Guinness, "Turning the Tables."

75. Guinness, "Turning the Tables."

76. Guinness, "Turning the Tables."

in finding ways that worldviews are false, and if there is a worldview that passes all the tests, then it is highly probable the worldview is true.

Still, there may be worldviews that twist themselves in such ways as to appear to meet all three tests, so Norman Geisler added two further tests that will get beyond some whimseys to find whether or not a worldview is true or false.

The Unaffirmability and Undeniability Tests

There is a possible shortcoming to the three tests. First explained by Norm Geisler in the first edition of his apologetics book, he develops the notion of two further tests. Due to their unique presuppositions, some philosophical systems may technically pass the tests and still be false—Hinduism is one such example. But they still fall out of the bounds of logic when further tested and are found to be indefensible. Hinduism's belief that there is no distinction between the material world and the ultimate, impersonal reality of Brahman might try to sneak past the tests, but under further inquiry will be found to be ridiculous. The two tests that Geisler introduces to meet this particular problem are the unaffirmability and the undeniability tests.

Norm Geisler first explains that the unaffirmability of a belief or world-view does not mean that something is unsayable or unstatable because one can put even the illogical or the absurd to words.[77] The unaffirmability test is a test for falsehood. Any statement or belief that one asserts in a way that one cannot affirm is self-defeating. If one undermines the only basis on which one can affirm the belief, that belief is rightly rejected.[78] Unaffirmability does not mean there is an absolute necessity for an empirical verification to affirm the belief's truthfulness (or even for a belief to assert anything factual at all) as A. J. Ayer would require (although the test would include empirically verifiable propositions).[79] It would also include logical principles and other a priori propositions (which Ayer would dismiss as a tautology).[80] This criterion tests a statement of belief expressing some fact that, upon reflection, defeats itself (and thereby one cannot affirm empirically or logically) and would thus lead to the natural conclusion that the belief is false. For example, making the statement, "I cannot speak a word

77. Geisler, *Christian Apologetics*, 1st ed., 141 .
78. Geisler, *Christian Apologetics*, 1st ed., 142.
79. Ayer, *Language, Truth and Logic*, 36.
80. Ayer, *Language, Truth and Logic*, 76.

of English," is not affirmable (since logically, one makes the statement in English) and is, therefore, self-defeating and false. An agnostic or skeptic in their worldview says, "I know that I cannot know anything about reality," which is not affirmable (since there is a knowledge of a lack of knowledge) and is therefore self-defeating and thereby false.

The undeniability test suggests that if something is undeniable, it logically must be true.[81] To deny the undeniable is self-defeating. So, for example, if I state as one of my worldview beliefs that I deny my own existence, I fail the undeniability test because I deny that which is inherently undeniable—I have to exist in order to give a denial of my existence. I may deny something in the belief, but what I state defeats itself—my existence is undeniable. Another example is a belief that there are no such things as three-sided triangles. Triangles, by definition, have three sides—so a three-sided triangle is undeniable. To say a triangle has four sides is self-defeating since a triangle undeniably has three sides. Any worldview that includes beliefs affirming the unaffirmable or denying the undeniable is false. While these tests do not necessarily demonstrate the truthfulness of a worldview nor add to one's proofs or evidence in defense of a worldview, these are important truths in determining the falseness of a belief or worldview. Just because a worldview avoids these pitfalls does not make it true. Yet if a worldview affirms the unaffirmable or denies the undeniable, it is logically inconsistent and false. Therefore, these tests might not do much on their own, but in conjunction with the other tests, they help in the apologetic endeavor.

Conclusion

The three tests based on the three basic epistemological theories of truth (along with the added tests of unaffirmability and undeniability) offer a reliable means to test worldviews for truthfulness and falsity. When one filters the significant beliefs of any worldview through these tests, one can determine if the worldview itself holds up to scrutiny. Any worldview with several foundational beliefs that fail these tests is then open to rejection. At the same time, any worldview whose beliefs pass these tests has the highest probability of being true and right, and the individual would do well to consider embracing such a worldview seriously.

The combination of tests proposed by worldview apologists might appear to fit under a form of combinationalism—combining numerous

81. See Geisler, *Christian Apologetics*, 1st ed., 143–45.

methods into one single model.[82] As such, one might raise several criticisms that are placed against combinationalism for these sets of tests as well. For example, some may argue that a combination of tests that in themselves are inadequate cannot merge to form an adequate test for truth.[83] Similar to the leaky bucket criticism discussed in chapter 3, one may give a similar answer—the three tests for truth (with the addition of unaffirmability and undeniability) do not have the same flaws. One test undergirds the weaknesses of the other tests, such that they miss nothing (or, to stay with the metaphor, nothing leaks).

Another criticism is that the model presupposes what entails the concept of fact and truth within the framework of the truth theories and tests.[84] In other words, all the concepts with which this model works are themselves worldview-dependent. I would respond that these tests are both objective and inescapable—a belief or system of beliefs, to be accepted as making a statement about truth, must be consistent with irrefutable laws of logic (the law of non-contradiction is inescapable), consistent within itself (otherwise it destroys its own foundation), have some correspondence with reality (otherwise it is mere fantasy), have practical application (otherwise it is theoretical fancy), and must avoid self-defeating premises. These are not worldview-dependent; they are the reality of existence.

Geisler mentions the criticism that combining truth-tests at best tests for falsity, but not the truth, since more than one worldview may in some way consistently and adequately meet the original three tests.[85] This critique might have some validity to a point. Hence Geisler enjoins the tests of unaffirmability and undeniability. The contentions of the apologetic are that the worldview that meets all the tests has a higher probability of truth than any other, so it is accurate to state that the tests seek the truth. They do not merely exist to prove a worldview false.

These tests are not necessarily perfect since they do not bring one to a perfect certainty, only that the worldview whose beliefs pass the tests has the highest probability of being correct. However, again, that does not invalidate this apologetic approach. Even as Geisler himself admits, there is no perfect system that gives an undeniable test for truth, writing, "For one thing, no finite mind is in actual possession of *all* the facts. Further,

---

82. Geisler, *Christian Apologetics*, 2nd ed., 105.

83. Geisler, *Christian Apologetics*, 2nd ed., 116.

84. Geisler, *Christian Apologetics*, 2nd ed., 117.

85. Geisler, *Christian Apologetics*, 2nd ed., 118.

no finite person is able to comprehend completely *all the facts*. Also, finite minds have difficulty in understanding the consistency and inconsistency between all the facts. For these reasons, absolute certitude will be difficult, if not impossible, for every opposing truth claim made within a given worldview. As in almost everything else in life, probability is the guide. However, in some cases of high probability one may reach a level of moral certitude in which, while other views are logically possible, there are no known reasons to veto the acceptance of the truth claim being adopted."[86] Whatever conclusion one makes from these tests (that fit the known facts) brings them closer to the truth about the various worldviews. The next chapter demonstrates how this is the case.

86. Geisler, *Christian Apologetics*, 2nd ed., 134. Emphasis original.

5

Putting Worldviews to the Test

"The best way to destroy your enemies is to
make them adopt your worldview."

—BANGAMBIKI HABYARIMANA,
The Great Pearl of Wisdom

Four Basic Questions of Life

THE TESTING OF WORLDVIEW truthfulness takes place within the context
of how a worldview answers life's ultimate questions.[1] Francis Schaeffer
notes that the underlying beliefs for each worldview (whether religious or
philosophical) deal with the same questions, but each worldview gives different answers and uses different terms.[2] If a worldview cannot adequately
address and answer the crucial issues with which humanity wrestles, or the
answers it provides are not logically consistent, empirically adequate, and
experientially relevant, then the worldview cannot be truthful.

Among worldview scholars, there is no consensus about what life
issues constitute an appropriate paradigm for testing—or at least no consensus on how the categories are labeled. For example, Perry C. Cotham

1. Cotham, *One World, Many Neighbors*, 18.
2. Schaeffer, *He Is There and He Is Not Silent*, 279.

groups life's great questions under seven broad headings: (1) The Absolute, (2) The World, (3) Humans, (4) The Problem of Evil, (5) The Better Life, (6) Community and Ethics, and (7) Interpretation of History.[3] James Sire tests and compares worldviews according to eight basic questions: 1) What is prime reality—the really real?; 2) What is the nature of external reality, that is, the world around us?; 3) What is a human being?; 4) What happens to a person at death?; 5) Why is it possible to know anything at all?; 6) How do we know what is right and wrong?; 7) What is the meaning of human history?; and 8) What personal, life-orienting core commitments are consistent with this worldview?[4] Tawa J. Anderson, W. Michael Clark, and David K. Naugle analyze worldviews through four questions: (1) What is our nature?; (2) What is our world?; (3) What is our problem?; and (4) What is our end?[5]

Another angle taken for worldview truth-testing and analysis is following the biblical categories of creation-fall-redemption (CFR). Christian scholars see this as the natural progression of the biblical narrative. For example, J. Mark Bertrand describes this paradigm as the

> way of seeing the story of Scripture, a trajectory with three points: creation, fall, and redemption. Like many churchgoers, I was accustomed to thinking of these as doctrines, not chapters in a story, but a subtle shift in thinking made all the difference. The Bible opens with a story about the creation of the world. . . . That story is followed closely by a narrative about the fall. . . . The rest of the Bible recounts the unfolding of that elliptical promise, the coming of a Messiah who will restore what was broken in the fall. Redemption, planned from eternity, enters time in the person of Jesus Christ. All history before the cross looks forward to it, just as all history since looks back upon it. Creation, fall, and redemption are the story of the Bible, but they are also the story of the world in which we live. It is our story. The gospel is a proclamation that God has made good on his promise, that the old enemy, Death, has been defeated by Christ, and if we are in Christ we live in hope of resurrection. This is a starting point, a belief system and a story all at once. It tells us who made us, what's become of us, and what's in store for us.[6]

3. Cotham, *One World, Many Neighbors*, 18–19.

4. Sire, *The Universe Next Door*, 22–23.

5. Anderson, Clark, and Naugle, *Introduction to Christian Worldview*, 18.

6. Bertrand, *Rethinking Worldview*, 103–4.

In his dissertation on worldview analysis, Bryan Billard Sims lists scholars such as Hermann Dooyeweerd, Francis Schaeffer, Albert Wolters, and Nancy Pearcy, among others, who advocate this CFR paradigm. Yet, he also admits that as of the writing of his dissertation, no one had "specifically developed the Christian worldview with these elements for apologetic purposes, specifically interacting with alternative religions."[7]

Sims defends the CFR matrix by arguing that these are the decisive turning points in salvation history—these events altered not only redemptive history but also world history, and the categories comprehensively encompass human history.[8] He argues that the CFR matrix is a legitimate paradigm for the analysis and testing of worldviews since, in some way, all worldviews recognize that life came from somewhere, that there is chaos or problems in this life, and they offer a solution of some sort. While these are distinctly biblical categories, other worldviews would not necessarily follow the flow of this paradigm—a Hindu, Buddhist, Muslim, or Secular Humanist would not necessarily think along the lines of these concepts. Therefore, when interacting with someone from a non-Christian worldview, the apologist would not necessarily persuade them with a redemptive model to demonstrate their worldview's falseness and Christianity's truthfulness. There are, however, general life questions (that still envelope these groups) that are common to all worldviews and create a shared context for worldview analysis and truth-testing.

There are four fundamental questions that humans ask themselves that all worldviews answer to some degree. Origin: Why do I exist and how did I come into existence? Meaning: What is the meaning of life and how do I find purpose? Morality: How do I determine what is right and wrong, good and evil? Destiny: What happens when I die and to what end or purpose is the world headed? No matter what worldview a person embraces (be they pantheist, atheist, polytheist, or theist), they must answer these four questions in some way since these are the basics of human existence. So, at these points, a person tests the truthfulness of their worldview, and the worldview of others, for logical consistency, empirical adequacy, and experiential relevance. A worldview's answers to these questions must offer a coherent system that corresponds with reality in such a way that one can live out the consequences of its beliefs.

---

7. Sims, "Evangelical Worldview Analysis," 130–33.

8. Sims, "Evangelical Worldview Analysis," 133–34.

It should be carefully noted that worldviews must pass the tests of truth across these four categories. It is not enough for a worldview to pass the tests of truth in one category only to fail at one or all of the other three. For a worldview to be true, it must be logically consistent, empirically adequate, and experientially relevant in its corporate treatment of origin, meaning, morality, and destiny. And the conclusion that one will draw after such analysis is that only the Christian worldview can stand the test of time and give the ultimate answers to such deep life questions.

Theologians and apologists have utilized similar questions or categories (or nuances of these four) in their analyses. James Orr believes that as the mind seeks a belief system to make sense of the world, it pursues answers to these same questions—questions that he sees reason itself bringing to the consciousness of the individual. He writes, "On the theoretical side, the mind seeks unity in its representations. It is not content with fragmentary knowledge, but tends constantly to rise from facts to laws, from laws to higher laws, from these to the highest generalisations possible. Ultimately it abuts on questions of origin, purpose, and destiny, which, as questions set by reason to itself, it cannot, from its very nature, refuse at least to attempt to answer. Even to prove that an answer to them is impossible, it is found necessary to discuss them, and it will be strange if, in the course of the discussion, the discovery is not made, that underneath the profession of nescience a positive theory of some kind after all lurks."[9]

Arlie J. Hoover also recognizes that while there may be many ways to analyze worldviews, the best approach is to show how the worldviews answer certain basic metaphysical questions, which the questions of origin, meaning, morality, and destiny closely represent.[10] Several other theologians defend using these questions as the context for worldview apologetics. Melvin Tinker believes these four categories touch upon the total human experience, giving a fitting assessment to any belief system that seeks to make sense of life.[11] William Brown views these four as the ultimate questions for life and provides a defense for why these are the most appropriate categories by which to compare worldviews, stating,

> These are ultimate for basic reasons. First, they are inescapable. Every person has to answer these questions in one way or another. Secondly, the answers to these questions touch every single

9. Orr, *Christian View of God*, 6–7.
10. Hoover, *Dear Agnos*, 55–56.
11. Tinker, "Reasonable Belief?" 349.

molecule of the universe. Thirdly, they are ultimate because the answers affect you. And fourthly, they are ultimate because there are answers. That's why I want a worldview that fits the world. I want what's true. I want to know why we are here. I want to know how we know what is right and wrong. . . . But considering these questions is what makes us human. And the reality is that they are interconnected. When you answer one, you really answer the others as well. When you answer the question about origin with "God created everything," you've answered why we're here, how we know what's right and wrong, and what happens when you die. They are interconnected.[12]

For these reasons, I agree that the questions of origin, meaning, morality, and destiny are the appropriate context by which to test and compare the varied worldviews. To elaborate, I briefly describe the areas of life these questions envelope before demonstrating how one could utilize this approach for particular select worldviews.

Origin

Since it is about beginnings, the question of origin is often the first set of questions for which a person seeks answers, or they are the commencing questions a worldview answers by its beliefs. People want to know why there is something rather than nothing and how that something came into existence. These are no mere theoretical inquiries of armchair philosophers. These are deep, personal questions because the answer to the question of the origin bears a heavy weight on the other three questions as well as on one's conception of one's being.

This category includes the big questions of where the universe came from (be it earth and heavens, stars and planets, time and space). However, it also touches on the origins of humanity—was humanity created or a cosmic accident? Does man have a soul and body, or merely a body? Deep metaphysical, ontological, and epistemological questions are laid bare in this category. What is the nature of reality? What is the ultimately ultimate? This category even gets very personal as it asks of a worldview what it even means to be human, which then often leads one to ask: why am I here? What is the nature of being, and how is it that humanity has the capability of knowledge?

12. Brown, "Thinking Worldviewishly," 12–15.

Meaning

This category answers where a worldview places the value of existence. Where does one go to find the meaning and purpose for life? What makes someone valuable? What is the basis of the belief that all lives are valuable? One worldview might say that humans have no essential worth or ultimate purpose, while another might say that humanity has a calling and purpose granted to them by a deity. Which, if either, is true? Which worldview is consistent in its dealings with meaning, and are the answers it gives livable in the world? This category is the most personal of all because it not only asks why a person exists but then, ultimately, who cares? Is the value of something or someone inherent, or is value acquired? According to a worldview, why should someone love or be loved? Does anything in the universe have any worth, and if so, where does that worth come? The question even touches upon aesthetics as it asks what beauty is. Who or what determines what is beautiful? What is the purpose of the aesthetic? What does it add to existence?

Morality

The category of morality discerns how a worldview determines the distinction between right and wrong. Where does a worldview receive its ethical framework? What exists that leads the human mind to form an "ought" out of what "is"? What is the basis for moral decisions? Who determines the difference between good and evil? What is the standard and who or what establishes that standard? When one does not meet the standard, are there consequences and who hands out those consequences? What laws, commands, principles, rules, or dogmas lead and guide humanity under which they have a moral obligation? Are those standards, laws, commands, principles, rules, or dogmas livable or merely an ideal? What is pleasure and when does one's seeking for personal pleasure begin to infringe on the rights of others? Does humanity even have rights, and if so, from where do they come? Who determines who has rights and who does not? Who has the power to take away those rights and under what circumstances?

This category not only touches upon chosen ethical systems but also asks questions about what is wrong with the world and humanity and the solution to what is wrong. From where comes the corruption of the universe? Who defines this corruption? What determines what is corrupted and unnatural and what is not? What is the recourse to that corruption? This category also places an obligation upon a worldview to answer the great questions of evil and suffering—what is it, where did it come from, what is the solution, and what is the meaning behind it?

Destiny

The final category of questions is that of destiny. Why do people die and what happens when they die? Is there life after death? Is there a heaven or hell or limbo or nothingness? Are there eternal rewards and punishments? Who determines who receives rewards and punishments? Is there an eternity and what is it? Will there be justice where wrongs are righted, or will there be no recourse? Where is the universe headed? What will be its end?

The various worldviews may not answer every question under each category, but they will have answers for the big questions. Within this context, a truthful worldview will be logically consistent, empirically adequate, and experientially relevant across all four categories. If a worldview falters in any of these categories, then it is false.

Analysis of Worldviews in Light of the Tests and Questions

It would be impossible for a project like this to take every worldview to the tests of truth or even to make a complete analysis of the few worldviews with which I interact. What I present is but the bare bones of how one may analyze and critique worldviews. Neither do I claim to interact with the best representation of each group. Nevertheless, examining a sample of worldviews that represent the significant categories of belief systems is crucial to demonstrate how the worldview apologetic approach functions. First, analyzing representative atheistic, theistic, and pantheistic systems that contradict the Christian worldview, I finally bring Christianity under the scrutiny of these tests, following the four questions of origin, meaning, morality, and destiny as closely as possible. Admittedly, so much more could be done. But I hope it gives a small sample of what is possible.

Naturalistic Humanism (Contradictory Atheistic System)

Atheism as a category speaks of a worldview that disbelieves in the existence of a God, gods, or any supernatural being who has relations to or interactions with the known universe. The term itself is wide-ranging, and several subcategories of worldviews could fall under its nomenclature (for example, some may categorize specific atheistic systems as agnosticism, skepticism, postmodernism, or rationalism). Still, others distinguish between mythological atheism, dialectical atheism, and semantical atheism.[13] A good representative of atheism, which also seems to be one of the most vocal opponents of Christianity, is naturalistic humanism (also termed modern humanism, scientific humanism, democratic humanism, and at times secular humanism, which is a term I avoid because of the cultural and political ramifications often associated with it). Corliss Lamont defines this worldview as a "naturalistic philosophy that rejects all supernaturalism and relies primarily upon reason and science, democracy and human compassion."[14] Although the worldview claims that science compels them toward a materialistic view of the universe, some adherents, such as Richard Lewontin, are truthful enough to admit that no matter where logic or empirical evidence may lead, they will begin with the material presupposition and not stray. He writes, "It is not that the methods and institutions of science somehow compel us to accept a material explanation of the phenomenal world, but, on the contrary, that we are forced by our *a priori* adherence to material causes to create an apparatus of investigation and a set of concepts that produce material explanations, no matter how counter-intuitive, no matter how mystifying to the uninitiated. Moreover, that materialism is absolute, for we cannot allow a Divine Foot in the door."[15]

Naturalistic humanism claims that the known universe is all that exists without any outside help or influence. Nature and the physical universe are the totals of reality, are closed and uniform systems of material causes and effects, and are entirely self-contained and self-sufficient. As such, atheists perceive that one could conceivably know the whole of reality through scientific investigation and the use of reason.[16] While relying heavily on the influences of science and philosophy, and apparently having an answer

13. Geisler and Watkins, *Worlds Apart*, 46–47.
14. Lamont quoted in Kumar "Humanism Philosophy," 81.
15. Lewontin, "Billions and Billions of Demons," 31; Emphasis original.
16. Samples, *A World of Difference*, 203.

for life's ultimate questions, one finds that it fails the truth-tests in many areas. Naturalistic humanism vehemently denies that there is a God who created and sustains the known physical universe. Instead, they believe that the universe randomly formed itself or always existed, ignoring the consistency problem of explaining how humanity can make order from a random universe. As such, they undermine the foundations of the rationality and science they hold dearly.

One variation of naturalistic humanism believes that the universe started independently, having come from nothing. This group usually holds to the scientific theory commonly referred to as the Big Bang Theory. While the science itself may or may not be wrong, their interpretation of it has serious problems. They cannot explain the existence of anything, be it real or theoretical. The scientific laws they hold so dear did not previously exist, so how can one know if they are reliable now if they are nothing but the product of chance? They have yet to explain how matter can suddenly pop into existence. They cannot explain how something can come from nothing just "out of the blue." They cannot answer the question of origins because any explanation they give comes from a reasoning that has no basis if it just appeared randomly. In other words, for a worldview to state that everything is explainable by science or reason, they have yet to explain scientifically or rationally how something (the universe) can come from nothing. The mathematical chances of the universe coming from nothing and randomly forming life are near impossible. Donald Page of Princeton's Institute for Advanced Science has calculated "the chances of 'the creator sticking in a pin' and pulling out just this combination of qualities that make such a unique universe are way beyond astronomical," one out of $10,000,000,000^{124}$—a number that exceeds all imagination.[17]

Another variation of naturalistic humanism states that the universe has always existed—matter is eternal. However, the science to which they subscribe would say otherwise. The laws of thermodynamics demonstrate the universe's expansion and movement toward a state of equilibrium, all indicating that it had a beginning.[18] Yet, one of atheism's foundational scientific theories, the Big Bang Theory, says that the universe has a beginning, which means that it could not have existed eternally. From their worldview, this physical, concrete reality has no way of explaining its own existence. Thus, naturalism's own pet scientific theories undercut its empirical

17. Marlow, "Third Loyola Conference on Quantum Theory."
18. See, for example, Craig, *Reasonable Faith*, 140–50.

adequacy. "If the standard Big Bang model is true, then the universe is not eternal; it began to exist at some point in the finite past. If whatever begins to exist has a cause and if the universe began to exist as the Big Bang model suggests, then the universe must have a cause. This cause by necessity is beyond the physical universe."[19] Norm Geisler and William Watkins also argue that one can only explain a finite, contingent object if there is an infinite, intelligent cause. Chance does not explain the origin of the universe's existence.[20] Even its philosophical advocates, like Bertrand Russell, have difficulty explaining the universe's origin through this worldview—indicating that the universe needs no explanation when he says, "I should say that the universe is just there, and that's all."[21] However, that is merely an explaining away of the serious question at hand.

Not only is naturalistic humanism's explanation for the origin of the universe fraught with difficulties, but so is its explanation of the origin of humanity. Clinging to Darwin's evolutionary natural selection, they ignore the lack of empirical evidence (such as lack of observable evolutionary events or lack of fossil evidence) as well as the rational hurdles of explaining how something contingent can exist without a cause. Darwin's evolutionary theory is just that—a theory. It is devoid of solid scientific proofs (especially using their own definitions of science) and is philosophically untenable. Again, the mathematical chance that their explanation for the origin of humanity happened as they report is beyond what even their own sciences accept. Fred Hoyle and N. C. Wickramasinghe found that the odds of forming a single enzyme from amino acids anywhere on our planet's surface by random trial are 10^{20}.[22]

As recent scientific studies have demonstrated, naturalism's evolutionary theories cannot even explain the origin of one organ in living creatures, much less the origin of the creatures in totalities. Darwin himself admits that "if it could be demonstrated that any complex organ existed, which could not possibly have been formed by numerous, successive, slight modifications, my theory would absolutely break down."[23] Scientists such as Michael J. Behe take up Darwin's challenge and demonstrate that there are such organs, offering better alternatives to Darwin's theory. Behe

19. Anderson, Clark, and Naugle, *Introduction to Christian Worldview*, 249.

20. See Geisler and Watkins, *Worlds Apart*, 61–71.

21. Copleston and Russell, "Debate on the Existence of God."

22. Hoyle and Wickramasinghe, *Evolution from Space*, 24.

23. Darwin, *Origin of Species*, 87.

introduces the concept of irreducible complexity, where "a system has a number of components that interact with each other, and if any are taken away the system no longer works."[24] What Behe proposes is that there are organs and organisms that could not work without all the parts working at the same time, therefore they could not have evolved from simpler organisms or systems—the human eye being one such organ. That being the case, macroevolution is impossible, Darwinism is false, and design becomes a better explanation. Although this in itself is not necessarily a smoking gun, it is one piece demonstrating that naturalism is left wanting.

Alvin Plantinga also offers an interesting insight into naturalism's evolutionary claim for humanity's origin. He notes that naturalism and evolution do not give an explanation as to why one can hold his or her beliefs or cognitive functions as reliable. He contends that one cannot solely argue that the reliability of beliefs is dependent on a resulting behavior since there is no satisfactory naturalistic explanation for a causal connection between the two. Plantinga maintains that the probability of the naturalistic explanations for relying on one's beliefs is inscrutable. This leads to a skepticism toward any beliefs produced by one's cognitive faculties since the beliefs are no more likely to be true or false. However, not only is there skepticism about one's beliefs but there is also then a skepticism about one's doubts about one's beliefs since these doubts also are dependent on one's beliefs. This then naturally leads a naturalist to be skeptical about their beliefs about naturalism itself. Therefore, naturalism is self-defeating.[25]

C. S. Lewis offers a similar assessment. Lewis notes that to understand naturalism, one must look at it as a total system (a worldview), and within its system, naturalism refutes itself. He argues that naturalism discredits reasoning to a place where it no longer supports the worldview. Naturalists must argue that rational thinking came from the evolutionary process of natural selection. This gives no basis to believe that one's thinking process can actually give insight that one could call true. If the thinking process is nothing more than chemical, there is no reason to suppose that the beliefs produced by that chemical process are valid. There is no necessity to accept an argument trying to demonstrate the soundness of an argument when the process of producing the argument itself is suspect. Naturalists give no rational case that supports making a logical jump from cause to effect or from grounds to consequent. They have no support or explanation on

24. Behe, "Evidence for Design," 119. See also Behe, *Darwin's Black Box*.
25. Plantinga, "Evolutionary Argument against Naturalism," 9–14.

how one can know something or make an inference about something.[26] As James Sire notes, "If my mind is conterminous with my brain, if 'I' am only a thinking machine, how can I trust my thought? . . . These and similar questions do not arise from outside the naturalist worldview. They are inherent in it."[27]

Due to these shortcomings, naturalism is then difficult to live out consistently. Although naturalists believe the universe exists by random chance, they do not live as if the universe exists by random chance. In everyday life situations, naturalists act as if there is order in the universe and the universe has a basis of absolute truth. John Frame gives an example, writing,

> John Cage, the composer, [is] a man whose philosophy says that all is chance—randomness—a philosophy that he seeks to express in his music. But as an amateur mushroom-grower, Cage does not abide by his philosophy of chance. Rather, he presupposes an order, a world of law. Some fungi are mushrooms, others toadstools, and it matters which ones you pick to eat! Thus Cage is unable to apply his philosophy of randomness to all of life; he cannot live with it. This fact casts doubt on whether he really believes it or not. I would say that he believes it, but not strongly or consistently; he also holds other beliefs inconsistent with this one. . . . Thus he is not able to apply his unbelief to all the areas of his life."[28]

As Tommy Allen indicates, "The inconsistency of the Naturalist worldview as [normally defined] cannot give an account for the use of reason, explanation, interpretation, certainty, and the intelligibility of anything."[29]

The problems with naturalism's explanation of origin reverberate into the other important areas of life as well. If they cannot confidently answer why something exists rather than nothing (and, therefore, life is a cosmic accident with no purpose), neither can it explain personality, reality, or morality. A universe and a humanity that are impersonal since they have no cause appear to demonstrate that nothing and no one matters—nothing has value, no one has meaning. Bertrand Russell explains,

> Man is the product of causes which had no prevision of the end they were achieving. . . . His origin, his growth, his hopes and fears, his loves and his beliefs, are but the outcome of accidental

26. C. S. Lewis, *Miracles*, 17–36.

27. Sire, *The Universe Next Door*, 93.

28. Frame, *Doctrine of the Knowledge of God*, 149–50.

29. Allen, "Transcendental Argument."

collocations of atoms . . . no fire, no heroism, no intensity of thought and feeling, can preserve an individual life beyond the grave . . . all the labours of the ages, all the devotion, all the inspiration, all the noonday brightness of human genius, are destined to extinction in the vast death of the solar system, and . . . the whole temple of Man's achievement must inevitably be buried beneath the debris of a universe in ruins—all these things, if not quite beyond dispute, are yet so nearly certain, that no philosophy which rejects them can hope to stand."[30]

James Sire argues that the issue of meaning and value is troublesome for the naturalist since their explanation of the universe's origins and humanity give no explanation for why one ought to consider humans valuable. The best naturalism can offer is the claim that humans are unique, but gorillas and every other category of nature is unique in itself. Beings that appear by chance have no claim to any value or worth.[31] Of course, some have no problem with this purposelessness of naturalism. Peter Atkins writes, "Science has no need of purpose . . . all the extraordinary wonderful richness of this world can be expressed as growth from the dunghill of purposeless interconnected corruption."[32]

The meaninglessness of life and existence echoes very hollowly in the hearts and minds of most people, making this worldview hardly livable, yet it is the inescapable consequence of a random existence. Every individual has their own personality, but science has yet to explain how such personality comes from non-personality—how the personal can come from the impersonal. This lack of explanation leaves a barrenness of soul and uncertainty of existence, with an underlying message that life is nothing more than mere futility. Although they make lofty claims, their worldview leads to a pointless and hollow existence.

Their worldview puts them in the problem of being unable to justify their beliefs. For example, they may try to proclaim all humanity's equality, yet their worldview undercuts their claim. Vince Vitale observes, "For all people to have equal value, there has to be something about each human person that is equally true and that cannot change. What is it? Any naturalistic answer to this question will not do, because our natural endowments are distributed along a spectrum. Some are less intelligent than others, less

---

30. Russell, "A Free Man's Worship," loc. 501–8, Kindle.

31. Sire, *The Universe Next Door*, 93.

32. Atkins, "Limitless Power of Science," 127–28.

healthy, less useful for society, less good looking, less wealthy, less capable of passing on their genes, less moral. Even if currently you measure up well by some of these standards, one day you won't. We will age, we will weaken, and our financial worth will fluctuate. . . . By any naturalistic standard, human value is fleeting and graduated, with some coming out less valuable than others."[33] Try as it might, naturalistic humanism cannot explain or justify or sustain the existence of such human virtues as love and beauty and liberty and justice—those that demonstrate purpose, value, and worth.

However, the naturalists will not concede so readily. Having no point of reference to give anything meaning or purpose, this worldview finds that it must come up with its own meaning as best as it can in the circumstances in which it finds itself. I would say that naturalistic humanism has to "fake it" since it can give no reason that anything or anyone has value or worth. If matter is all that exists, nothing has intrinsic worth. The consequence of this is nihilism—nothing has validity, nothing has meaning, everything is just there.[34] Nihilism leaves human beings as nothing more than "conscious machines without the ability to affect their own destiny or do anything significant; therefore, human beings as valuable beings is dead."[35] Naturalistic humanism eventually leads to nihilism because the worldview "does not supply a basis on which a person can act significantly. Rather, it denies the possibility of a self-determining being who can choose on the basis of an innate self-conscious character."[36] This is problematic since it is unlivable. "People cannot consistently live out nihilism; no one can live day to day with the affirmation that everything is meaningless."[37]

Nevertheless, naturalistic humanism appears to allow that these valueless beings (who are the epitome of nature's accidental existence) are the sole determiners of that which is right or wrong. However, there can be no morality without value. Morality is woven in with personhood, but if personhood has no value, neither can there be morality. If there is no moral lawgiver who has worth and gives worth, then any moral system has no worth. With the denial of transcendent value, there is no consistency in this worldview's beliefs about truth and ethics, and as such, their morals are hardly livable. Their morality leaves more questions than it gives answers.

33. Vitale, "Pluralism," 123.

34. Sire, *The Universe Next Door*, 94.

35. Sire, *The Universe Next Door*, 100.

36. Sire, *The Universe Next Door*, 102.

37. Anderson, Clark, and Naugle, *Introduction to Christian Worldview*, 252.

Numerous ethical systems and theories could fit under naturalism's broad spectrum. One example is the utilitarianism of John Stuart Mill, where "actions are right in proportion as they tend to promote happiness, wrong as they tend to produce the reverse of happiness . . . pleasure, and freedom from pain, are the only things desirable as ends."[38] The problem, however, is that one could use these ends to justify almost any means. Under this system, Hitler could justify the Holocaust because of the glorious end of having a pure Arian race. Another naturalistic ethic is Ayn Rand's objectivist ethics, where value is "that which one acts to gain and/or keep in the face of alternatives."[39] A person's life is the standard, so whatever they deem necessary to further that life is good, and reason is the means toward that goal. One's happiness is paramount, primarily found in productive achievement. The problem is that, while Rand may maintain that there would be no conflict between rational people's interests, it does leave open the possibility of conflict when one person's life-goals run opposite of another's life-goals. In such a case, whose life-goals win?

Winfried Corduan argues that naturalistic values have several problems. One problem is that within a naturalistic system, the values by which they live are arbitrary since a universe governed by chance can only produce chance occurrences. Any "law" that they posit (be it scientific or ethical) is a generalization on how the universe usually operates, but given the randomness of chance, there is no guarantee that the universe is always found that way. Another problem is that even if a naturalist could discover ways to describe how the universe operates accurately does not then automatically necessitate how things ought to be. The descriptive data of the universe does not justify any particular prescriptive moral law.[40] C. S. Lewis argues that, since naturalists have no basis for reasoning, then moral ideals deconstruct to mere illusions or biological by-products. An irrational and non-moral universe cannot lead to a moral judgment—there is no basis for forming an ought from what is. Naturalists may argue that moral ideals are formed under the influence of natural selection when the resulting behavior causes certain benefits to the species. However, this excludes any basis for it being a moral judgment—one cannot say that the belief or behavior is "right" or "wrong."[41] As Allen asks, "If morals are simply chemical conditions and

38. Mill, *Utilitarianism*, loc. 104–11, Kindle.
39. Rand, "The Objectivist Ethics."
40. Corduan, *No Doubt about It*, 86–88.
41. Lewis, *Miracles*, 53–60.

random collisions of protons and neutrons, by what standard can the Naturalist argue that natural disasters, children dying, victims of cancer, and ten million Ukrainians slaughtered in World War II are acts of immorality?"[42]

Similarly, Phillip Johnson finds that naturalists lack a way of justifying the imposition of obligations on others. Johnson bases his arguments on those given by law professor Arthur Leff. Leff argues that there can be no normative system of ethics based on anything other than human will, which might be disconcerting to many naturalists. His reasoning is that: "(a) all normative statements are evaluations of actions and other states of the world; (b) an evaluation entails an evaluator; and (c) in the presumed absence of God, the only available evaluators are peoples, then only a determinate, and reasonably small, number of kinds of ethical and legal systems can be generated."[43] If man, though, ultimately determines the rules, what happens when rules conflict with one another? Whose ethics and ideals will win? As Johnson then argues, without an authoritative evaluator, there is no way to distinguish between right and wrong—people just make it up. Johnson then adds his own argument that as naturalists might attempt to use logic for their moral cause, they never reach a foundation for their ethic. Johnson reasons that logical arguments cannot justify their own premises, so a different logical argument must be used to justify the previous argument's premises. However, that second logical argument cannot justify its premises, which will then go on ad infinitum. There is no way of coming to a starting point by which to found one's morals in a naturalistic way. Naturalists' reasoning power and moral assumptions ultimately find no basis.[44]

Still, naturalistic humanists decry the evils of the world. However, with their complaints and criticisms of a world gone wrong (for which they have no reason or answer), they miss the inconsistency of their belief. If a naturalist believes there is evil, they assume there is a form of good. But if there is a good, it has to have a basis somewhere. Good comes from a moral law, but a moral law does not happen by itself. A moral law comes from a moral lawgiver, but the naturalist denies this. Therefore, they undermine their ability to make any moral claim. This leaves the naturalist with no consistent or livable answer for what is right or wrong, much less for why there is even the existence of good and evil. Even an ardent follower of naturalism such as Bertrand Russell has difficulty explaining why people

42. Allen, "Transcendental Argument."

43. Leff, "Unspeakable Ethics, Unnatural Law," 1233.

44. Johnson, "Nihilism and the End of Law," 19–25.

embrace this worldview's view of morality while having no basis for it. He writes, "I cannot believe that values are simply a matter of my personal taste and so I find my own views actually quite incredible and I do not know the solution."[45] Moreover, atheist Kai Nielsen had to conclude that mere reason could not give moral direction when he writes, "We have not been able to show that reason requires the moral point of view or that all really rational persons, unhoodwinked by myth or ideology, should not be individual egoists or classical amoralists. Reason doesn't decide here."[46]

As indicated in the first chapter, several of this worldview's adherents blame religion for the ills and evils of this world. If any such wrongs came from supposed Christian sources, they did so despite the teachings of Christ, not because of them. Christ never advocated unjust war or injustice, or intolerance. On the other hand, one could argue that whatever evil came from the hand of those holding to the naturalistic worldview came as a consequence of the worldview itself. For example, a survivor of the gas chambers of Nazi Germany, Viktor E. Frankl, recognizes that the consequences of this naturalistic worldview have grave moral consequences, where he muses,

> If we present a man with a concept of man which is not true, we may well corrupt him. When we present man as an automaton of reflexes, as a mind-machine, as a bundle of instincts, as a pawn of drives and reactions, as a mere product of instinct, heredity and environment, we feed the nihilism to which modern man is, in any case, prone. I became acquainted with the last stage of that corruption in my second concentration camp, Auschwitz. The gas chambers of Auschwitz were the ultimate consequence of the theory that man is nothing but the product of heredity and environment; or as the Nazi liked to say, "of Blood and Soil." I am absolutely convinced that the gas chambers of Auschwitz, Treblinka, and Maidanek were ultimately prepared not in some Ministry or other in Berlin, but rather at the desks and lecture halls of nihilistic scientists and philosophers.[47]

The argument that such violence is the consequence of the worldview's beliefs is not merely some form of reductio ad absurdum but the logical and practical outworking of the worldview itself. Having survived the Russian Communist Revolution, Aleksandr Solzhenitsyn recognizes that the

45. Russell, "Letter to the *Observer*."
46. Nielsen, "Why Should I Be Moral?," 90.
47. Frankl, *The Doctor and the Soul*, xxvii.

"failings of human consciousness, deprived of its divine dimension, have been a determining factor in all the major crimes of this century. . . . Only a godless embitterment could have moved ostensibly Christian states to employ poison gas, a weapon so obviously beyond the limits of humanity."[48] Such evil regimes exist in naturalism because they have no foundation or point of reference for good, leaving no room for the value of humanity.

This worldview has no basis on which to build a moral system, yet they loudly pontificate the values of a naturalistic, secular society. Still, it collapses from having no foundation upon which to set it. They have nothing upon which to build a consistent, coherent, livable ethic. Yet, even when one demonstrates that their moral basis has no basis, they inconsistently cling to their natural law. They recognize a natural law at work in the making of the universe, but they deny a natural law at work in ethics, for to accept the latter might open the door to the possibility of the reality of the person of God. Yet it appears inconsistent to see law and order in the one but then deny its existence in the other realm. We find that an empirically inadequate origin births an unlivable view of meaning, leading to an inconsistent view of morality.

Finally, this worldview has no real answer for humanity's destiny. If the material is all that exists, then man has no soul or spirit. In their view, when a person dies, they cease to exist. This cessation of existence leaves no hope—no hope for righting wrongs, no hope for a meaningful end, no hope for transcendent existence. One loses much of life's purpose and meaning when one's destiny goes no further than six feet underground. A worldview that cannot adequately account for origin and purpose must keep quiet about destiny. However, the naturalist must ask themselves, what if they are wrong? Since their worldview is wrong about origin, meaning, and morality, what if it is wrong about destiny as well? If one clings to such a worldview to the end, only to learn too late of their mistake, there is no changing their beliefs. If the atheistic humanist is wrong, they lose everything.

This small analysis of an atheistic system barely scratches the surface but gives a brief insight into why this worldview is logically inconsistent, empirically inadequate, and experientially irrelevant. David Berlinski finds the worldview lacking in truthfulness, writing,

> Has anyone provided proof of God's inexistence? Not even close. Has quantum cosmology explained the emergence of the universe or why it is here? Not even close. Have our sciences explained why

48. Solzhenitsyn, "Men Have Forgotten God."

our universe seems to be fine-tuned to allow for the existence of life? Not even close. Are physicists and biologists willing to believe in anything so long as it is not religious thought? Close enough. Has rationalism and moral thought provided us with an understanding of what is good, what is right, and what is moral? Not close enough. Has secularism in the terrible 20th century been a force for good? Not even close to being close. Is there a narrow and oppressive orthodoxy in the sciences? Close enough. Does anything in the sciences or their philosophy justify the claim that religious belief is irrational? Not even in the ball park. Is scientific atheism a frivolous exercise in intellectual contempt? Dead on.[49]

As Arlie Hoover summarizes, "*The miracles of science are irrelevant to the truth of naturalism as a metaphysic.* The idea that nature is the sum of reality, that it is impersonal and non-axiological, and that it is eternal can't be proved empirically by any science or by any combination of sciences or by all the sciences put together."[50] Still, a world that clings to such a worldview has severe consequences, leading toward an unlivable philosophy where the reasoning and rationality it leaned upon gives way to the reality of what is truly going on with the human condition.

Islam (Contradictory Theistic System)

With Islam and Christianity both being found within the theistic category of worldviews, one would expect many similarities for some of the foremost issues of life. While there are some similar claims, the differences shine even brighter as Islam struggles with several tests for truth. Like Christianity, Islam believes that there is one God who is all-powerful, all-knowing, self-sufficient, ever-present, and absolutely sovereign.[51] Surah 47:19 of the Quran states, "So know that there is no god but Allah . . . and Allah knows the place of your returning and the place of your abiding." Surah 59:22–23 says, "He is Allah besides Whom there is no god; the Knower of the unseen and the seen; He is the Beneficent, the Merciful. He is Allah, besides Whom there is no god; the King, the Holy, the Giver of peace, the Granter of security, Guardian over all, the Mighty, the Supreme, the Possessor of every greatness Glory be to Allah from what they set up (with Him)." For Islam,

---

49. Berlinski, *The Devil's Delusion.*

50. Hoover, *Dear Agnos*, 58. Emphasis original.

51. Netland, *Dissonant Voices*, 83.

this god was never begotten and will never beget, and never has and never will have any associate with him in the godhead.[52] Surah 112:1–4 states, "Say: He, Allah, is One. Allah is He on Whom all depend. He begets not, nor is He begotten. And none is like Him." Therefore, unlike Christianity, there is no Trinity but one god with one personality. Allah's absolute oneness is such that he has no separation or differentiation in his mind, will, and actions.[53] Some sects of Islam so try to protect Allah's monotheistic nature that they even deny him having separate attributes.[54] It is precisely because of this "vigilant commitment to an absolute form of monotheism . . . that any attempt to identify God with another being or finite creature is viewed as blasphemy or idolatry (shirk). To do so is regarded as one of the worst sins in Islam."[55] Thus, they deny the possibility of Jesus Christ being God.

In their worldview, Allah created and sustains the known universe and has complete sovereign lordship over its affairs. Humanity is the pinnacle of everything that Allah created, into whom Allah breathed his spirit, to whom also Allah granted a vice-regency over the earth. Nevertheless, even having this higher status over the rest of creation, humanity is little more than a slave—created for Allah's service and worship.[56] All people are born with some knowledge that Allah exists. Allah created humanity with a nature that is more good than it is evil and thereby can perfectly obey him if so chosen. Islam does believe in the sin of Adam, but Adam's disobedience came from Satan's temptations and Adam's imperfections. Thus, Adam's sin did not transform or corrupt human nature; instead, it only affected Allah's original couple, whom Allah forgave when they repented. For Islam, sin "is more a weakness, defect, or flaw in human character rather than the radical corruption of human nature."[57] Thus, everyone throughout history up to the present day is born with an innate ability to both obey or disobey Allah and repent if needed.[58]

Many of Islam's beliefs are somewhat consistent with Christian accounts of origins, and one could defend their interpretation of origins with

52. Murray, "Islam or Christianity."

53. Murray, "Islam or Christianity."

54. Anderson, Clark, and Naugle, *Introduction to Christian Worldview*, 308.

55. Samples, *A World of Difference*, 249.

56. Anderson, Clark, and Naugle, *Introduction to Christian Worldview*, 294. See also Clark, "Islam," 23–24.

57. Netland, *Dissonant Voices*, 89.

58. Anderson, Clark, and Naugle, *Introduction to Christian Worldview*, 296.

similar argumentations and evidence utilized by Christian apologists. Yet, it is in other areas where the tests of truth help in constructive analysis, highlighting the problems with the Muslim faith. For example, there are inconsistencies between Muslim claims and historical evidence. The Quran, their source of authority that claims to be a historical document, denies the crucifixion and death of Jesus Christ. Surah 4:157–58 states, "And their saying: Surely we have killed the Messiah, Isa son of Marium, the messenger of Allah; and they did not kill him nor did they crucify him, but it appeared to them so (like Isa) and most surely those who differ therein are only in a doubt about it; they have no knowledge respecting it, but only follow a conjecture, and they killed him not for sure. Nay! Allah took him up to Himself; and Allah is Mighty, Wise." However, countless sources verify the crucifixion and death of Jesus Christ—many of which are not Christian, with Roman, Greek, Jewish, and Christian historians recording the crucifixion and death of Jesus. For example, the Roman historian Tacitus in his *Annals*, speaks of "Christus [who] suffered the extreme penalty during the reign of Tiberius at the hands of one of our procurators, Pontius Pilatus."[59] The Jewish historian Josephus records, "Now, there was about this time Jesus, a wise man, if it be lawful to call him a man, for he was a doer of wonderful works—a teacher of such men as receive the truth with pleasure. He drew over to him both many of the Jews, and many of the Gentiles. He was [the] Christ; and when Pilate, at the suggestion of the principal men amongst us, had condemned him to the cross, those that loved him at the first did not forsake him."[60] However, Islam's own authority denies the historical evidence. In conjunction with this, since they do not believe that Jesus died on the cross, they deny that He rose from the dead. Thus, their claims conflict with reasonable historical evidence and arguments. Islam's worldview does not correspond with the existing empirical proofs (some of which were mentioned in Chapter 3). As Netland summarizes, "The differences between Muslims and Christians, then, over the person and work of Jesus of Nazareth are fundamental and cannot be casually dismissed."[61]

These historical conflicts also unearth minor inconsistencies within the Quran itself. The Quran, Islam's holy book, denies that Allah would allow anyone to kill his prophets, with Jesus being a recognized prophet. However, elsewhere the Quran acknowledges that the unbelieving Jews

59. Tacitus, *The Annals*, 15.44.

60. Josephus, *Antiquities of the Jews*, 18.3.63–64.

61. Netland, *Dissonant Voices*, 93.

killed Allah's prophets. For example, Surah 3:183 states, "Those are they who said: Surely Allah has enjoined us that we should not believe in any messenger until he brings us an offering which the fire consumes. Say: Indeed, there came to you messengers before me with clear arguments and with that which you demand; why then did you kill them if you are truthful?" Another inconsistency is the doctrine of abrogation. Islam claims that the Quran is the unchanging authority for all the earth. For example, they claim that Allah gives a promise to protect his Quran from error and changes over time in Surah 15:9, "Surely We have revealed the Reminder and We will most surely be its guardian." However, by following the doctrine of abrogation (where later pronouncements of the prophets declare null and void earlier pronouncements), they demonstrate the exact opposite. Surah 2:106 states, "Whatever communications We abrogate or cause to be forgotten, We bring one better than it or like it. Do you not know that Allah has power over all things?" On the one hand, the Quran claims to be a perfect revelation, but on the other hand, it says that it can be changed by the whims of the moment. If any or all of the Quran is open to abrogation, then nothing was true to begin with. What is to say that other teachings, rules, or doctrines have not changed over time?

The Muslims' high claims for the Quran are suspect themselves. Muslims claim that the Quran they have today is precisely as Muhammad received it without any changes or corruptions made to the text. Winfried Corduan finds this claim questionable in two ways. First, there is the historical fact that Uthman, the third caliph, destroyed all copies of the Quran except the one he claimed to be authentic. This begs the question, what evidence is there that Uthman kept the right one? Second, Corduan notes that several textual variations have appeared, which calls into question any claim that there are no changes made to the text.[62]

In addition, Islamic theology teaches that their beliefs are a part of and dependent upon the truth of biblical revelation, and the teachings of the Quran are justified within and built upon these works. But then, on the other hand, they claim that these same biblical documents are inadequate, incomplete, corrupt, and untrustworthy (due to doctrines such as the Trinity or the Incarnation), thereby undermining their own authority.[63] For example, the Quran first says in Surah 3:3 that Allah gave the Bible, stating, "He hath revealed unto thee (Muhammad) the Scripture with truth,

---

62. Corduan, *A Tapestry of Faiths*, 61.
63. Samples, *A World of Difference*, 257.

confirming that which was (revealed) before it, even as He revealed the Torah and the Gospel." Then Surah 2:75 states that the words were altered, "Do you then hope that they would believe in you, and a party from among them indeed used to hear the Word of Allah, then altered it after they had understood it, and they know (this)." This belief toward the biblical documents is inconsistent at best and logically incoherent at worst. Islam also offers no evidence or rationale to support the claim that the biblical texts are corrupt. Nevertheless, "it can be shown through the writings of the Christian church fathers that such doctrines as the Trinity and the deity of Christ (considered perversions by Muslims) actually had a very early origin in the history of Christianity and were drawn from the canonical writings produced by Jesus's apostles."[64]

The Quran contains theological inconsistencies about the person of Jesus. For example, they affirm Jesus' virgin birth but deny him as the Son of God. But this forces them to explain why the virgin birth has any importance. Surah 19:19–21 reports the announcement of Jesus' virgin birth: "He said: I am only a messenger of your Lord: That I will give you a pure boy. She said: When shall I have a boy and no mortal has yet touched me, nor have I been unchaste? He said: Even so; your Lord says: It is easy to Me: and that We may make him a sign to men and a mercy from Us, and it is a matter which has been decreed." So, even though Islam's belief in the creation of the universe and humanity has the capacity of using some of the same support as Christian claims, this worldview's conflict with historically empirical evidence and its inconsistency within its own source of authority is problematic.

Islam's view of humanity is also existentially unsatisfying when considering the meaning and purpose of humankind's existence. Although the pinnacle of Allah's creation, man is a slave to serve and worship him. Surah 51:56 states, "And I have not created the jinn and the men except that they should serve Me." Emphasis is placed on Allah's sovereignty over the will of man, although Allah does not necessarily have a fulfilling plan for the individual. Some Muslims claim that "the provision, life span, deeds, and ultimate fate in the Hereafter of every human being are written by the angels as soon as the soul is blown into the fetus. Our destiny was decreed for us even before we were born."[65] Allah did not make humanity in his image, nor does Allah seek a relationship with humankind. Surah 50:16–18 states,

64. Samples, *A World of Difference*, 259.

65. Parrot, *Reconciling the Divine Decree*, 6.

"And certainly We created man, and We know what his mind suggests to him, and We are nearer to him than his life-vein. When the two receivers receive, sitting on the right and on the left. He utters not a word but there is by him a watcher at hand." These verses indicate that Allah's close presence would threaten humankind; therefore, two angels must mediate his presence with man. There is no interaction between a benevolent deity and his creation—humanity has no meaning or purpose for life other than to obey Allah.[66]

The Quran outlines the moral system handed down by Allah by which man shall live. Islam does not center ethics on Allah's love for humanity or humanity's love for one another—instead, Allah has his law, and obedience is the only demand. Therefore, the love found in Islam "very much mirrors human expressions of love. We love those who love us; we love those who are lovable; and we lavish our affections and give of ourselves to those who love us. At best, we act lovingly toward strangers. But we do not love our enemies. We do not love the unlovable. Our love, in general terms, does not transcend the bounds of what is deserved."[67] The Quran defines the categories of good and evil, right and wrong, based on Allah's will. However, Allah's laws may appear arbitrary, and as mentioned in the discussion about abrogation, the law itself might change. This would make it difficult to know what law to follow, how to live, or how to choose between right and wrong. Corduan notes that it is precisely because the Quran does not explain how the individual should live out the faith that the Hadith, the acts and sayings of Muhammad, emerged.[68] Samuel Zwemer notes that in Muslim theology, "The words 'permitted' and 'forbidden' have superseded the use of 'guilt' and 'transgression;' the reason for this is found in the Koran itself. Nothing is right or wrong by nature, but becomes such by the fiat of the Almighty. What Allah forbids is sin, even should he forbid what seems to the human conscience right and lawful. What Allah allows is not sin and cannot be sin *at the time he allows it*, though it may have been before or after."[69]

So, the laws and morals of Allah do not flow from the character or attributes of Allah. Yet, the morals that do flow from Islam's Sharia law grate against the existential expectations of many. Under Sharia law, Muslims can beat women for talking to men or not wearing a headdress, behead

66. Murray, "Islam or Christianity."

67. Murray, "Islam or Christianity."

68. Corduan, *A Tapestry of Faiths*, 61.

69. Zwemer, *Moslem Doctrine of God*, 51.

non-Muslims, and molest certain kinds of children.[70] One could argue that Sharia law takes away more from human existence than it gives. Nonie Darwish writes, "Muslim societies have not contributed much to humanity, but have actually destroyed and sucked away the talent and innovation bit by bit from the nations they conquered. Contrary to conventional wisdom, it is not Arab talent that came out of the Middle East, but the talent of the great civilizations conquered by Arabs and their swords."[71] Islam acknowledges that man has the freedom and the capability to choose whether or not to follow that law. Yet, in the areas where Islam has political power, there is a compulsion to believe—there is no choice or freedom to do otherwise. Peaceful criticism of the worldview brings the fear of inciting violence. Even its own authority calls for slaying the unbeliever that will not convert. Surah 2:191 reads, "And kill them wherever you find them, and drive them out from whence they drove you out, and persecution is severer than slaughter, and do not fight with them at the Sacred Mosque until they fight with you in it, but if they do fight you, then slay them; such is the recompense of the unbelievers." Surah 5:33 states, "The punishment of those who wage war against Allah and His messenger and strive to make mischief in the land is only this, that they should be murdered or crucified or their hands and their feet should be cut off on opposite sides or they should be imprisoned; this shall be as a disgrace for them in this world, and in the hereafter they shall have a grievous chastisement." As Mark Coppenger notices, "With over a billion 'members,' this religion is typically totalitarian when in power, and it seeks to extend its power along with its numbers in every corner of the earth. Continual violence is performed in its name, and its record of wholesome accomplishment is meager."[72] This compulsion and violence are the consequence of a worldview that has a deity without love and a humanity without meaning.

Islam's belief about man seems inadequate and inconsistent with reality. "Lacking in Islam . . . are concepts of the radical depravity of human nature, the pervasive impact of sin and the complete inability of humankind to redeem itself from the bondage of sin."[73] Kenneth Samples rightly describes how their view of humanity falls short, writing,

70. See Darwish, *Cruel and Unusual Punishment*.

71. Darwish, *Cruel and Unusual Punishment*, 172.

72. Coppenger, *Moral Apologetics*, 134.

73. Netland, *Encountering Religious Pluralism*, 185.

Islam's view of man seems unrealistic and even naïve. According to Islam, human beings are born innocent with an unequivocally good and positive nature. The worst that can be said about people is that as finite creatures they are weak, limited, susceptible to temptation, and generally forgetful of God. . . . Individual people, Islam insists, are capable of living in obedience to God with his guidance. Yet, does this anthropological viewpoint comport with the reality of human experience? . . . The history of humanity—while having many intellectual, moral, and spiritual bright spots—is also filled with brutality, war, racism, and genocide. . . . Islam's high view of man also seems to run counter to its teachings about ultimate submission to God. If man's nature is good and humans are merely limited and weak, then why can't devout Muslims achieve moral perfection?[74]

While the Muslim ethic is to obey Allah, no one has been able to achieve such perfection, and Islam gives no answer as to either cause of disobedience, nor does it give humanity a path toward obedience.

What is Allah's response to man's disobedience? There is an inconsistency in the monotheistic Allah. Two of Allah's names in Islam are "The Just" and "The Merciful," meaning that Allah is both all-just and all-merciful. There can be no compromise on either of these. However, humanity is sinful and a lawbreaker. Islam acknowledges that the sin of humankind defaces the whole earth. As Murray then notices, "If God is maximally just, then he necessarily punishes sin. If God is maximally merciful, then he always wants to forgive it. But how can he do both without compromising either? One might say that God, as the Almighty, can just forgive sin as an exercise of sheer power. But this presents an incoherent view of omnipotence leading to logical absurdities, like saying that God has the power to create square circles or can cause himself to cease existing."[75] Where Christianity finds God in Christ being both Just and Justifier, Islam has no recourse. This lack of any advocacy leaves humanity in a lurch. Humanity must cleanse itself without any actual capacity to do so.

Regarding Islam's view of destiny, divine judgment comes on the basis that human beings are fully responsible for their actions. Since all human beings have chosen the road of disobedience out of their weaknesses, all human beings are subject to judgment. Muslims believe that before the end of days, the Mahdi will come as the final messenger of Allah to eliminate

74. Samples, *A World of Difference*, 261–62.
75. Murray, "Islam or Christianity."

Allah's enemies and usher in a brief time of universal justice. Then Allah himself will destroy the present world and inaugurate a final judgment to determine the eternal destiny of every human being.[76] However, there is little to no direction regarding where one ultimately lands for eternity. How much is too much disobedience? Do different sins weigh heavier on the scale than others? Islam believes in a heaven for the righteous and a hell for the unrighteous. However, what constitutes one over the other?

> It is a common belief that two angels follow each Muslim through-out life. The angel on the person's right records his good deeds, while the angel on the person's left records his bad deeds. In ef-fect, a person's destiny rests upon the preponderance of his actions as measured upon a scale. Generally speaking, Muslims have no assurance that they will earn paradise, but this dilemma often is understood as an incentive to strive for greater submission to God's laws. Paradise involves both spiritual and physical pleasures (often described in sensual terms for men), whereas hell consists of eternal banishment from God's presence accompanied by de-spair and physical punishment. While this judgment seems based solely upon a human being's actions, Muslims also believe that Al-lah consigns people to paradise or hell based upon his sovereign or arbitrary will."[77]

This worldview misses several components about destiny to make it viable. First, there is no consistent concept of forgiveness since no basis for forgiveness is given other than Allah's arbitrary will. Second, there is no concept of assurance. Corduan notes that Islam is a works-based religion that leaves adherents wondering how much is enough to earn heaven. No one can claim assurance of heaven since, in the end, it ultimately comes down to Allah's decree of who he believes deserves salvation.[78] Third, there is no concept of hope. There is not a Muslim (no matter how devout they think themselves to be) that can know whether or not their good deeds outweigh their bad, thereby whether or not they will go to heaven upon death. No matter how observant a Muslim might be, no matter the rules he keeps, there is still no guarantee of heaven or paradise. One's eternal destiny remains unknown until one gets there. One's fate is weighed in the balance of obedience and disobedience. There is no need for a Savior, and Islam

---

76. Corduan, *A Tapestry of Faiths*, 183–84. See also Netland, *Dissonant Voices*, 88–91.
77. Samples, *A World of Difference*, 252–53.
78. Corduan, *A Tapestry of Faiths*, 109 n. 4.

offers no salvation from one's sins and consequences.[79] Hopeless and help-less to do anything about it, Islam finds itself logically inconsistent, empiri-cally inadequate, and experientially irrelevant in life's important questions of origin, meaning, morals, and destiny.

Hinduism (Contradictory Pantheistic System)

Netland describes Hinduism as "a family of religious traditions that are the product of some 4,000 years of development."[80] Although Hinduism does not have a singular founder, authoritative text, or sect, there are several core beliefs to which they ascribe that make worldview analysis possible. It is a monistic worldview that believes all of reality is one—that which exists has no duality, plurality, parts, or distinctiveness.[81] All that exists is the ultimate, impersonal reality of Brahman. This is often described with the terminology that god and the universe are one. What appears to be an individual within the world is an atman, an emanating consciousness that is either identical to Brahman or at least a part of the Brahman.[82] Although there is no single authoritative story on when, where, or how the universe emanated from Brahman, adherents generally accept that the universe is some type of illusion or collective hallucination superimposed by the ulti-mate reality.[83] Hinduism is a form of pantheism, a belief that all is Brah-man (or in some sects, all is part of Brahman), and Brahman is all—the infinite, absolute, immutable, and indivisible.[84]

Therefore, according to this worldview, the universe and all its in-habitants do not exist in reality. Souls are merely illusory actors on an imaginary stage. While these souls play out the story in what looks like a world, truth and reality happen backstage, behind the scenes. Individual souls are not actually individual souls. Everything is Brahman through and through—the actors, the stage, the props. Even though each emanation of atman appears to have its own consciousness, that is nothing but an illu-sion. These atman have a problem in that they have forgotten from where

---

79. Netland, *Dissonant Voices*, 90.

80. Netland, *Dissonant Voices*, 41.

81. Samples, *A World of Difference*, 235.

82. Anderson, Clark, and Naugle, *Introduction to Christian Worldview*, 271–72.

83. Anderson, Clark, and Naugle, *Introduction to Christian Worldview*, 276.

84. Samples, *A World of Difference*, 235.

they originate, so what is called an existence is spent attempting to return (or be re-absorbed) into Brahman.

There are several issues metaphysically, ontologically, and epistemologically. First, the idea of Brahman is incoherent. Hinduism describes Brahman as having no attribute or properties—it is a pure undifferentiated Being. It is logically impossible for a Being to have existence yet have no properties. Not only must the Being have the property of existence, but it must also have at least another property that describes its existence. Also, when tied with the belief that Brahman emanates itself in several atman, it is logically absurd to claim that the property-less Brahman can project atman that have several properties.[85]

Next, there is incoherence and inconsistency with the atman and Brahman distinction (or lack thereof). Samples explains, "According to this form of Eastern monism, all reality is an undifferentiated one without any particular distinctions. Yet this philosophy identifies the distinct human self (atman) as being essentially one in essence with Ultimate Reality. This 'distinct true self' idea logically conflicts with monism's basic assertion that there are no distinctions. In other words, the critical concepts of monism and atman in the worldview of pantheistic monism contradict each other. The concept of atman affirms what monism denies."[86] There is an inconsistency in claiming that the soul is distinct from the all, yet in the same way, the soul is in complete union with the all. It is contradictory to claim in the same way and at the same time that the soul is both united and separated from Brahman. This explanation of human existence also fails the unaffirmability test. An adherent to this worldview has to claim that "I do not exist" since they are but illusory projections of Brahman. However, they would not be able to affirm this statement because they have to exist to claim not to exist. Therefore, their claims are incoherent and self-defeating. Related to this, it takes a reason and a will to recognize one's personal existence, which is indicative of a personality. Again, demonstrating incoherence, this worldview does not explain how an impersonal Ultimate Reality can project various atman, each with a unique personality.

Corduan also demonstrates a contradiction in Hinduism's description of existence. They claim that god and the universe are one. Hinduism's description of god/Brahman is that it is eternal, omnipotent, and unchanging. However, the universe is finite, temporal, limited, and changeable.

85. Netland, *Encountering Religious Pluralism*, 210.
86. Samples, *A World of Difference*, 240.

The universe did not always exist, but at some time for some reason the universe emanated from Brahman. Yet the two are still one—the infinite Brahman and the finite universe are indistinct. Corduan finds this to be a logical contradiction since something cannot be both finite and infinite at the same time in the same way.[87] Some Hindus may argue that the finite universe is illusory—it doesn't really exist. Corduan then gives an apt illustration to exemplify the logical absurdity when he writes,

> Let us consider Shirley MacLaine as she stands on the beach proclaiming, "I am God!" We would like to know, specifically, who is God? It cannot be the Ms. MacLaine who is a part of the finite world of appearance, for we just learned that this Ms. MacLaine can only be an illusion. So it must be the infinite God who is now announcing to the world something she has just come to realize, namely that she is God. This is absurd. The infinite cannot forget something and then learn it. It must have always been God and always known it. In short, for the finite Shirley MacLaine to claim that she is God is impossible; for infinite God to become Shirley MacLaine and learn that she is God is incoherent. It just does not make sense.[88]

In addition, Hinduism's concept of truth appears self-defeating. According to Netland, they believe in two levels of reality that offer two levels of truth. The higher truth of *para* is ultimate; then there is the lower truth of *apara*. Hinduism considers the lower truth from the lower reality to be illusion and ignorance. To find the higher level of truth, one must transcend the ordinary realm since nothing from the lower level of truth can actually confirm or deny it.[89] However, how can anyone accept Hinduism's view of ultimate reality with this view of truth since this world works on the lower level of truth? Why should anyone accept their claims about origin, meaning, morality, and destiny as true since these claims are illusory and ignorant? By their view of truth, they have undercut any claim to truth. Netland offers his own criticism. First, even though they deny that logical principles like the law of noncontradiction apply to the highest level of truth, they actually appeal to the law of noncontradiction by stating the distinction between the two levels of truth. Second, adherents cannot give reasons why one ought to accept this belief, for to do so would appeal to

87. Corduan, *No Doubt about It*, 93.

88. Corduan, *No Doubt about It*, 94.

89. Netland, *Dissonant Voices*, 148.

the rational and logical criteria that they deny can justify the assertion that ultimate truth transcends ordinary truth.[90]

This worldview's explanation of origin and existence also has problems with empirical adequacy. Hinduism offers no evidence that bases its claims in reality. Their monistic and pantheistic claims fly in the face of scientific discovery, human psychology, and everyday experience. How could a multitude of consciousnesses come from an impersonal reality along with a world that, by all appearances, is logical and reasonable? "The assertion that the material, physical universe is an illusion completely undercuts the correspondence test. The universe and an individual's conscious and empirical awareness of it strikes human beings as self-evidently real and true."[91]

These problems also extend to the areas of meaning and morality. If what appears to be individuals are nothing but projections, then each projection has no meaning or purpose for existence (since they do not really exist). This belief in humans being mere projections flies in the face of experience. How can an impersonal being project itself in billions of different ways, with each projection having its own hopes, dreams, and desires for a relationship? How can the impersonal even seek relationship or communion or union? The system somehow lets slip that humanity longs for a relationship with a transcendent personal other. Hinduism is known as a religion of millions of gods—someone to worship and to seek in the brokenness of existence. Why would projections seeking oneness with reality need to seek something outside itself (when supposedly there is no one besides one's self)? This worldview believes quite literally that all the world is a stage, and the roles of the actors are beyond their control but are moved by the being behind the curtain. One must ask, how can an impersonal reality have a will or a purpose that it imposes on its projections?

Amid these inconsistencies is a moral system tightly woven with its idea of destiny. For Hinduism, each life "is imprisoned in this eternal cycle of death and rebirth called *samsara* . . . [which] could be defined as the 'passing through or cycling through successive lives as a consequence of moral and physical acts.' Individuals accumulate karma through moral and physical acts . . . every action has a consequence that will affect this life and the next."[92] So, wherever a person finds themself in this particu-

90. Netland, *Dissonant* Voices, 149.

91. Samples, *A World of Difference*, 242.

92. Anderson, Clark, and Naugle, *Introduction to Christian Worldview*, 272–73. Emphasis original.

lar reincarnation is due to the choices made in the previous life. However, several inconsistencies immediately reveal themselves. First, how can an impersonal atman that changes from life to life still maintain its uniqueness from Brahman to have to pay for previous decisions? In other words, how can one atman die and cease to exist, only for that same atman to return in a different form when there is nothing but Brahman? Second, since having an infinite regress of lives is an impossibility, there must have been a first life.[93] How was the lot for that person in their first life determined if there was no karma for which it had to answer? Third, without any recollection from previous births, how would an atman know what not to do or what they need to do to make things right from a previous life?

Moreover, there are no set rules of right and wrong. Netland argues that Hinduism's concept of the two levels of truth and reality makes it impossible for them to make an objective distinction between good and evil, right and wrong.[94] Still, with whatever laws one might discern, breaking them is more akin to breaking the laws of nature than breaking the laws of a judicial system.[95] Whatever rules or laws one may claim for this religion often seem reprehensible. For instance, there is the caste system where individuals are born into a particular status in life, supposedly due to the karma of the previous life. Corduan says of the caste system, "The traditional Hindu society with its caste system is nothing if not institutionalized racism. They believe that God created the caste system and that the 165 million [untouchables] in India are justly consigned to their situation."[96]

Nevertheless, instead of doing good to help their fellow man in order to gain good karma, the higher castes treat the lower castes poorly and consider the no-caste untouchables as unclean. Are they not concerned about the karma they are accumulating in their present incarnation? India (where Hinduism has its highest population and the caste system still reigns) has some of the most abject poverty and suffering in the world. What one can make of a Hindu moral system is inconsistent and patently unlivable. For example, a story in some of Hinduism's sacred writings speaks of Krishna counseling Arjuna that killing his cousins is acceptable because he would only be killing their bodies, not their souls. And yet elsewhere, Krishna

93. See Craig, *Reasonable Faith*, 96–97, on why infinite regress is impossible.

94. Netland, *Dissonant Voices*, 190.

95. Corduan, *A Tapestry of Faiths*, 96.

96. Corduan, *No Doubt about It*, 261.

says not to kill animals because they have souls, again demonstrating some inconsistencies in this worldview.

Women also suffer under such a system where they have less value than men and are treated as inferior no matter their caste, which leads to long-standing subordination and oppression.[97] This is especially seen in the suttee, the ritual of burning widows on their husband's funeral pyre. Richard Grenier describes this horror, "In southern India the widow was flung into her husband's fire. In the valley of the Ganges she was placed on the pyre when it was already aflame. In western India, she supported the head of the corpse with her right hand, while, torch in her left, she was allowed the honor of setting the whole thing on fire herself. In the north, where perhaps women were more impious, the widow's body was constrained on the burning pyre by long poles pressed down by her relatives, just in case, screaming in terror and choking and burning to death, she might forget her *dharma*."[98]

What happens to these people deemed substandard is the consequence of the system itself; as Samples describes,

> The lower castes in that religious/cultural/societal structure have recognized that a reincarnation-based religious philosophy is practically unworkable, oppressive, and fatalistic in nature. Members of India's lower echelon are consistently marginalized in society, suffer stigma and discrimination, and feel trapped in a religious determinism beyond their ability to change. The practical fruit of reincarnation has proven quite sour in those parts of the world that take this philosophical system seriously. Reincarnation also proves to be a convoluted moral system. It claims that people suffer because of injustices performed in their past lives. However, this claim leads to monumental intellectual and moral problems. First, it means impoverished children living in India are suffering because of their past-life injustices. But if these children are reaping justice for their previous evil actions, then why would anyone want to help them? Why give them food, shelter, and clothing if such acts interfere with the just punishment they so rightly deserve?[99]

Moreover, the system has no recourse for the world's suffering. A system whose only answer to the question of the existence of evil and suffering is

---

97. Anderson, Clark, and Naugle, *An Introduction to Christian Worldview*, 274–75.

98. Grenier, *The Gandhi Nobody Knows*, 148. Emphasis original.

99. Samples, *A World of Difference*, 243.

that it is only an illusion of a schizophrenic entity has no existential usefulness for those who are experiencing the suffering.

Finally, this Hindu worldview offers no hope for the future that is experientially relevant. Hindus seek moksha—freedom from the cycle of rebirths to reunite with Brahman. There are three ways to attempt to obtain this: the way of knowledge, the way of works, and the way of devotion.[100] There is no assurance that someone will find these paths in any of their lifetimes. Even if they did find it, all it would lead to is an absorption into the impersonal Ultimate Reality. So, the only choices are to continue in the seemingly never-ending cycle of birth and rebirth or cease to exist. There is no hope in the cessation of existence, nothing to look forward to, no ultimate sense of justice for righting wrongs, and no ultimate meaning for a life well-lived. Thus, Hinduism as a worldview is left wanting.

Christianity

Having briefly surveyed how truth-tests demonstrate the falseness of other worldviews, one also observes that the truth-tests will demonstrate the truthfulness of the Christian worldview. Within the context of the four life questions, the answers of Christianity are logically consistent, empirically adequate, and experientially relevant.

The Christian worldview believes that there is one transcendent God who is eternal, all-powerful, all-knowing, and everywhere-present. This God, although having one nature and being, is comprised of three distinct personalities (a Trinity—Father, Son, and Holy Spirit). While apologetic arguments for centuries have reasoned toward this God as a First Cause (cosmological), a Grand Designer (teleological), and the Moral Law-Giver (moral), reason is not able to lead one to a Triune Being, nor would one be able to find empirical evidence to prove this as the case. While the doctrine of the Trinity is a mystery and seemingly paradoxical, it is not an outright contradiction. One nature with three persons (one What with three Whos) may be inexplicable, but it is not illogical. While Greek philosophers argued for centuries about the mysteries of unity and diversity in the universe, it comes from the nature of the Eternal One. This God, who himself has always existed and was never created, is the great Creator of all things that exist outside himself. There was an existence where nothing but God

---

100. Anderson, Clark, and Naugle, *An Introduction to Christian Worldview*, 278–81. See also Netland, *Dissonant Voices*, 49.

himself subsisted. God created the universe of space and time without any previously existing material (ex nihilo). He formed and filled the universe under his watchful care, which led to the pinnacle of his creation: humanity. God made humanity (both male and female) in his image, giving them a co-regency over the earth, with an order to fill and subdue it.

While this makes for a good story, is there logical, rationale, and empirical evidence that verifies such claims? Through the worldview apologetic approach, several strands of proofs demonstrate the truthfulness of these worldview beliefs. One area of evidence is scientific. There are four strong points of science that most naturalists would concede that point to the truthfulness of the Christian claims of a designed creation: 1) The universe had a beginning and did not create itself (according to scientific proofs discussed earlier); 2) The universe is knowable (otherwise science would be an impossibility); 3) The universe is regular (it follows set laws), and 4) the universe is finely tuned for life.[101] From whatever angle one might analyze the known universe, it always appears to point outside of itself. The universe is unable to explain its own existence. While not directly arguments for the Christian God, the Christian worldview makes sense of this line of evidence when placed in conjunction with further lines of evidence and argument.

One can find further evidence for the Christian worldview with its belief that man was a unique creation of God, not merely a product of random chance. Evolutionary chance cannot explain the specified complexity of some of the simplest forms of life or even one vital bodily organ, much less the entirety of a human being. Just consider the complexities of human DNA. Since random chance appears to be a statistical impossibility, the intelligent design of man and the universe seems a matter of course. Considering such arguments, former NASA Scientist Robert Jastrow observes, "The essential elements in the astronomical and biblical accounts of Genesis are the same: the chain of events leading to man commenced suddenly and sharply at a definite moment in time, in a flash of light and energy," and then later admits, "For the scientist who has lived by his faith in the power of reason, the story ends like a bad dream. He has scaled the mountain of ignorance; he is about to conquer the highest peak; as he pulls himself over the final rock, he is greeted by a band of theologians who have been sitting there for centuries."[102]

101. Vitale, "Scientism," 66.
102. Jastrow, *God and the Astronomers*, 14.

Moreover, skeptical scientist Francis Crick has to admit for himself, "An honest man, armed with all the knowledge available to us now, could only state that in some sense, the origin of life appears at the moment to be almost a miracle, so many are the conditions which would have had to have been satisfied to get it going."[103] Although not giving up on an evolutionary possibility, Crick would go on to state the sheer enormity of the task as he continues, "But this should not be taken to imply that there are good reasons to believe that it could not have started on the earth by a perfectly reasonable sequence of fairly ordinary chemical reactions. The plain fact is that the time available was too long, the many microenvironments on the earth's surface too diverse, the various chemical possibilities too numerous and our own knowledge and imagination too feeble to allow us to be able to unravel exactly how it might or might not have happened such a long time ago, especially as we have no experimental evidence from that era to check our ideas against."[104] Evolutionary explanations have a lot of hurdles to cross. The Christian theistic explanation is the most consistent and empirically adequate explanation both scientifically and rationally.

What also sets Christianity apart from most other worldviews is that it bases itself on history, opening itself up for empirical investigation for many of its primary claims—often confirmed by sources that are not sympathetic toward Christianity. Gary Habermas notes, "We should realize that it is quite extraordinary that we could provide a broad outline of most of the major facts of Jesus' life from 'secular' history alone. Such is surely significant."[105] Thus, Christian claims open themselves up to historical investigation. Significant events crucial to the worldview, such as the crucifixion and resurrection of Jesus, offer themselves for verification. When researched, one finds strong evidence pointing to their reality. For instance, Gary Habermas lists twelve points of historical fact pointing to the reality of the resurrection that I have referenced in Chapter 3. Kenneth Sample notes why such empirical evidence is important when he writes, "The truth-claims of Christianity are open to, and even invite, historical investigation. The key events of the life, death, and resurrection of Jesus Christ, the historical person, can be examined and thus are subject to verification or falsification. . . . The ability to objectively test a worldview's truth-claims is critically important in the overall consideration of truth.

103. Crick, *Life Itself*, 88.

104. Crick, *Life Itself*, 88.

105. Habermas, *The Historical Jesus*, 224.

Historic Christianity invites that type of investigation and scrutiny."[106] Thus, Corduan claims that "Christianity is the only religion whose truth depends strictly on historical claims."[107] Most of Christianity's significant doctrines depend on a correspondence with reality.

That there are historical evidence and arguments for essential Christian doctrines in no way declares that scholars have found empirical evidence for every single Christian belief or assertion or that they can logically deduce every point of theology. Nevertheless, due to the evidence that has made itself available, there is a strong correlation between Christian claims and truth. Samples again aptly summarizes,

> The realities of the world and life match what the Bible teaches about God's creating the universe. . . . Christian theism scores well on the basic correspondence test for several reasons. First, when the Bible discusses truth . . . it generally incorporates a correspondence theory (truth equals that which matches reality). Therefore, according to historic Christianity, beliefs that conform to reality must be embraced. Truth cannot be separated from reality. Second, the Christian theistic worldview affirms a type of scientific realism (believing the time-space-matter universe to be an authentic objective reality). Moreover, history proclaims Christianity's respect for the empirical facts of nature. . . . Third, in the Christian faith, unlike Eastern mystical religions, people can generally trust their experiences in life and in the world. And the encounters characteristic of human existence are consistent with, not contrary to, the faith. The Christian worldview doesn't separate faith from real-life experience.[108]

Moreover, because the Christian account of origins and historical realities is logically consistent and empirically adequate, the other areas of consideration are experientially livable.

Since Christianity claims that God made man in his image, this means that God has placed his own value and worth upon humanity. The individual, no matter any internal or external attributes or factors, has an intrinsic value God placed upon them that comes from outside themselves. Christianity claims that when Adam disobeyed God and plunged all of humanity into a sinful existence, the image of God was marred but not destroyed. Thus, humanity still has God's spiritual imprint upon them, giving them

106. Samples, *A World of Difference*, 272.

107. Corduan, *A Tapestry of Faiths*, 126.

108. Samples, *A World of Difference*, 271.

their essential worth. God bestowed upon humanity a dignity and purpose that nothing or no one else could have conveyed upon them, and thus, nothing or no one else can take that dignity and purpose away. However, another clue to the meaning of life, according to Christianity, is that God pursues a relationship with humanity, even in their fallen, sinful state. God does not stay distant and transcendent, but God comes near to man—so near that he himself took on humanity to restore the relationship that sin stole away. Moreover, with the relationship offered through Jesus Christ, he then provides a relationship via the indwelling of the Holy Spirit. God relates to everyone as an individual, uniquely made and uniquely called, having a purpose for each of them—a purpose realized upon acceptance by faith.

Christianity bases its categorization of morals on the reality of God— good and evil are what they are based upon God's standards which God based on his character. He is the indicative that justifies the imperative—from him comes the "ought" because of who he "is." Humanity existentially experiences this truth whenever they attempt to categorize right and wrong or try to explain the existence of evil. As argued by many apologists, if there is evil, there is good; if there is good, there is a moral law; if there is a moral la,w there is a moral lawgiver. Christianity posits that God is the Moral Lawgiver.

There are two particular strengths to Christianity's moral claims. First, Jesus Christ himself exemplified the morals perfectly, setting the example for those who would follow him. No other worldview has a founder or leader that not only pontificated its ethical system but also lived it out in the open for all to see. Even Pontius Pilate had to declare that he found no guilt in Jesus (Luke 23:4). Skeptic W. E. H. Lecky takes notice when he writes, "The character of Jesus has not only been the highest pattern of virtue, but the longest incentive in its practice, and has exerted so deep an influence, that it may be truly said that the simple record of three short years of active life has done more to regenerate and to soften mankind than all the disquisitions of philosophers and all the exhortations of moralists. This has indeed been the wellspring of whatever is best and purest in the Christian life."[109] Then those who follow in His footsteps, no matter how imperfectly they may try, still enjoin a changed life that reverberates to those around them.

Second, God's moral laws for humanity make sense not only in light of humankind's meaning but also in his sinfulness. Humanity, made in the image of God, has essential value, so morality reflects the sacredness of human life. To say that the actions of a Hitler against humanity are

109. Lecky, *History of European Morals.*

wrong is to make a judgment of ethics based on that essential worth of man found only in the Christian worldview. However, to admit such a moral law is also to admit that humanity falls short of that moral law. What makes Christian ethics a testable truth is that Jesus Christ alone explains the human condition that corresponds with reality—humankind is fallen, broken, and sinful, but also too weak to change the state in which they find themselves. Jesus gives the most logically consistent and empirically adequate description of man because this is every person's lived experience. Malcolm Muggeridge is quoted as having said, "The depravity of man is at once the most empirically verifiable reality but at the same time the most intellectually resisted fact."[110]

Quite often, Christianity's opponents will raise the issue of evil's existence as an objection to this worldview, arguing that if there indeed is a God like Christians proclaim and describe, then there ought not to be evil in the world (or so much gratuitous evil, as some frame the argument). Since evil exists, there cannot be a good, all-powerful God. J. L. Mackie argues that the premises of God being omnipotent, God being wholly good, and yet evil still exists entails a contradiction. If two of the premises are true, then the third premise must be false. He believes a problem lies in the fact that theologians must adhere to all three beliefs but cannot do so consistently or logically.[111] There is not necessarily a logical inconsistency to there being both a Christian God and evil. One can make several retorts to the objection: evil exists because of humanity's free will, God uses evil to transform man's moral and spiritual character, or God uses it to bring about a greater good.[112] For example, Alvin Plantinga offers a free will defense against Mackie's claims. He argues that a world is more valuable when it contains creatures who are significantly free to perform their actions than if the world did not contain said creatures. God has the ability to create such creatures, but if He does so, He cannot cause them to do only what is right because if He did, they would no longer be free. To create creatures that can choose the morally good, they must also be capable of doing that which is morally evil (without God's interference to prevent them from doing so). That creatures choose moral evil does not count against God's omnipotence or goodness because the only way to have prevented the moral evil would

110. Long, "Undeniable Depravity."
111. See J. L. Mackie, "Evil and Omnipotence," 200–212.
112. Samples, *A World of Difference*, 269.

be to remove the moral good.[113] However, by raising the question, they imply there is an ultimate standard of goodness, and there is something wrong in the world that falls short of that goodness. The Christian worldview's treatment of destiny gives the only remedy to this problem that is both livable and hopeful.

Christianity communicates that humanity cannot overcome their sin and brokenness, but instead, through the death and resurrection of Christ, God offers forgiveness as a gift that one receives by faith. One cannot reach a spiritual apex, follow a rule, or perform a ritual to reach God. Instead, God reached down to humanity. In almost an ironic fashion, "the greatest act of evil on humanity's part (the crucifixion of God in human flesh) resulted in the greatest good for humankind."[114] Here God placed his justice upon another to demonstrate his mercy. God does not compromise his character and offers the only provision for humankind's common spiritual malady.

With the offer of forgiveness also comes the provision for humanity's common physical malady—death. As Jesus conquered the grave and rose from the dead, so he offers freely to others the hope of a life that does not end—both an eternal spiritual life and then a resurrected physical life. His own physical resurrection offers proof of the physical resurrection he offers to others. The hope of all humankind rests on an empirically verifiable fact. The problem of death and life after that, for which all worldviews must answer, finds its most logical and hopeful answer in Christ—hope that is both in the present and reaches the future. This hope permeates every belief in the Christian worldview and answers every question of life. Without the resurrection, Christianity would not stand. One might argue that the resurrection is the linchpin for the entire worldview apologetic endeavor. It answers humanity's greatest problem in a logically consistent and empirically verifiable way, allowing one to have a faith that is livable.

By way of summary for testing the Christian worldview, it alone answers the questions of origin, meaning, morality, and destiny in ways that are logically consistent, empirically verifiable, and existentially livable. When placed in comparison with other worldviews, be they atheistic, pantheistic, or theistic, only Christianity gives a realistic accounting of the human condition and still offers people genuine meaning, purpose, and hope both in this life and in the life to come.[115] Those espousing a Christian

---

113. Plantinga, *God, Freedom, and Evil*, 29–34.

114. Samples, *A World of Difference*, 269.

115. Samples, *A World of Difference*, 274.

worldview may not have all the answers, but one finds that apologetics done within the sphere of worldviews that tests for truth and falsity demonstrates that Jesus, in the historical reality of His life, death, and resurrection, is not only the way and the life, but He is the truth.

6

Apologetics at Work

"Apologists should have calluses on their brains from thinking, on
their hands from serving, and on their knees from praying."

—CHRISTOPHER BROOKS,
*Urban Apologetics: Answering Challenges
to Faith for Urban Believers*

A Practical Scholarship

APOLOGETICS IS NOT MERELY an academic exercise where one debates issues without concern for the outcome of the interchange; instead, apologetics is an evangelistic and discipleship tool for heart and mind change. I believe a lot of the criticism toward apologetics stems from the belief that apologetics is the end game. It never has been and never will be. I am in total agreement with Francis Schaeffer's thoughts on the matter. He writes, "Apologetics, as I see it, should not be separated in any way from evangelism. In fact, I wonder if 'apologetics' which does not lead people to Christ as Savior, and then on to their living under the Lordship of Christ in the whole of life, really is Christian apologetics. There certainly is a place for an academic study of a subject called 'apologetics,' as the defense and the credibility of Christianity, but if it does not lead the students to use that material in the way I have spoken about in the previous sentence, one can ask its value."[1] As I mentioned in the first chapter, apologetics is the means to the end. It is the machete that chops through the thick jungle of a false worldview while at the same time creating a path to the gospel. And Schaeffer himself demonstrated how his worldview apologetic style informed his evangelistic style.

> How this practically worked itself out in the life of Schaeffer was that in his evangelism and presentation of Christianity he would not begin with "accept Christ as Savior;" instead he would begin where Scripture begins, starting with the doctrine of God, establishing the worldview structures of Christianity grounded in the doctrine of creation, revelation, and the historic fall, and then and only then move to redemption, pointing people to the Lord Jesus Christ, who alone is their only hope. Why? Because, like Paul in Acts 17, he knew that unless he first developed a biblical frame of reference, i.e., worldview, the proclamation of the gospel would not make sense and his hearers would not then hear the gospel for what it truly is, in its own categories and on its own terms. Schaeffer, like Paul, was very concerned that the gospel is not wrongly dismissed or reinterpreted into another alien worldview framework, for that only leads to a distortion of the gospel message. And especially in our pluralistic, postmodern, inclusive age, in order to present Jesus Christ as not just another god or savior, but the exclusive Lord, Savior, and Judge, Schaeffer saw that it was imperative to build a biblical-theological framework, rooted in the story line of Scripture. That is, he saw that it was crucial to think in a worldview manner, rooted and grounded in the God who is there.[2]

Schaeffer believed that the evangelism that emanates from apologetics should touch all of reality and all of life. That means that portraying this apologetic method merely through intellectual or scholarly debate, while important, is not the exhaustive process. The apologetic can be demonstrated through sources that involve every aspect of a person's normal, daily existence. Yes, we can touch the mind by intellectually demonstrating whether a worldview passes the tests through abductive means, but there are other avenues to analyze the belief systems and interact with their ideas rather than merely scholarly and philosophical. Schaeffer believed that ideas reach areas such as art and music and the culture in general, as well

---

1. Schaeffer, *God Who Is There*, 186–87.
2. Wellum, "Ideas Have Consequences," 50.

as the philosophical and theological.[3] It would only make sense to engage the worldview through these areas as well. We can take off the roof of false worldviews and build bridges for gospel presentation, engaging in these (and even more) areas where worldviews put themselves on display. A song or a painting can cause an inner reflection about what one believes as much as an argument. Often, through these mediums, people came to their worldview to begin with. It would only seem natural that one could use them to challenge the worldview. Through their particular forms of expression, the artist tells a story—giving a narrative about reality through symbols that relate to the great questions of life and teach a way of being in the world.[4] A. Steven Evans recognizes how a good story is a catalyst for a change of mind and life. He writes, "Careful attention must be given to the role of oral tradition and the impact it has on cultural transformation, since it holds the key to catalyze worldview and cultural transformation effectively."[5] For many who take their emotions as the starting point for determining beliefs, giving themselves over to whatever the artist or storyteller is peddling is like grabbing the hand of truth. We should at least extend the right hand to them. But for this to be effective, the roof must be blown off of a false worldview to build the bridge to the only true worldview.

Therefore, the scholarly is never set to the wayside. The scholarly side is used to enhance the evangelistic side. Schaeffer would not have it any other way, writing, "What I am saying is that all the cultural, intellectual or philosophic material is not to be separated from leading people to Christ. I think my talking about metaphysics, morals and epistemology to certain individuals is a part of my evangelism just as much as when I get to the moment to show them that they are morally guilty and tell them that Christ died for them on the cross. I do not see or feel a dichotomy: *this* is my philosophy and *that* is my evangelism. The whole thing is evangelism."[6] That is Christian love at work. "If we love men we shall have the courage to lift the roof off other people's lives and expose them to the collapse of their defense . . . .The more comprehending we are as we take the roof off, the worse the man will feel if he rejects the Christian answer."[7] One can take the roof off an opposing worldview by demonstrating that their worldview cannot hold up

3. Schaeffer, *God Who Is There*, 8.

4. Stewart, "N. T. Wright's Hermeneutic," 156.

5. Evans, "Matters of the Heart," 186.

6. Schaeffer, *God Who Is There*, 186.

7. Schaeffer, *God Who Is There*, 144.

to the scrutiny and then build the bridge by working out the implications of the Christian worldview, which has implications for all of life.

Belief That Gives Direction

The ultimate goal, however, is not only to question false worldviews and create an evangelistic opportunity. What the apologist is seeking is that everyone would believe in Jesus Christ and recognize his sovereign control over every aspect of life. One not only grasps the Christian worldview but lives out its implications. This is the true outcome of evangelism and discipleship—to believe in Jesus and to live for Jesus. As Schaeffer explains,

> Evangelism is primary, but it is not the end of our work and indeed cannot be separated from the rest of the Christian life. We must acknowledge and then act upon the fact that if Christ is our Savior, he is also our Lord in *all* of life. He is our Lord not just in religious things and not just in cultural things such as the arts and music, but in our intellectual lives, and in business, and in our relation to society, and in our attitude toward the moral breakdown of our culture. Acknowledging Christ's Lordship and placing ourselves under what is taught in the whole Bible includes thinking and acting as citizens in relation to our government and its laws. Making Christ Lord in our lives means taking a stand in very direct and practical ways against the world spirit of our age as it rolls along claiming to be autonomous, crushing all that we cherish in its path.[8]

When one determines a worldview is logically consistent, empirically adequate, and experientially relevant, the only reasonable reaction is for it to have a say in every area of life. If someone will claim the Christian worldview, then Jesus is Lord over everything. To do or say otherwise would be to live inconsistently with what one claims to believe. Martin Luther purportedly declares, "If I profess with the loudest voice and clearest exposition every portion of the truth of God except precisely that little point which the world and the devil are at that moment attacking, I am not confessing Christ, however boldly I may be professing Christ. Where the battle rages, there the loyalty of the soldier is proved and to be steady on all the battlefield besides is mere flight and disgrace if he flinches at that one point."[9]

8. Schaeffer, *The Great Evangelical Disaster*, 322.
9. Federer, *Great Quotations*.

But the very fact of the lordship of Christ also then informs our apologetic. "Christianity is truth for every area of life, so we should be prepared to answer questions in every area of life—we should not pretend that the Bible gives all the answers, but it does give the important ones. This includes philosophical questions. Christians should not be afraid of philosophy, only of practising philosophy independently of the Bible, which is rationalism."[10] The Christian worldview, and therefore the lordship of Christ, touches upon areas like environment, art, culture, history, law, ethics, sexuality, and politics. Consequently the Christian apology has something to say about these things as well. With this in mind, "Christians should be out in the midst of the world as both witnesses and salt, not sitting in a fortress surrounded by a moat."[11] Francis Schaeffer modelled this for us. "Schaeffer was known for teaching that the Christian worldview—and it alone—could undergird the full range of human life. What a person believed about Jesus Christ affected that person spiritually, morally, rationally, aesthetically, and relationally. What a society believed about Jesus Christ affected that society in all of its doings—economic, political, ecological, and so forth."[12] The Christian worldview not only contains the truth but also has meaning in everyone's present life, and the apologetic approach ought to draw this out. As Schaeffer himself notes, "As I rethought my reasons for being a Christian, I saw again that there were totally sufficient reasons to know that the infinite-personal God does exist and that Christianity is true. In going further, I saw something else which made a profound difference in my life. I searched through what the Bible said concerning reality as a Christian. Gradually I saw that the problem was that with all the teaching I had received after I was a Christian, I had heard little about what the Bible says about the meaning of the finished work of Christ for our present lives. Gradually the sun came out and the song came."[13] My desire is that by taking off the roof and building the bridge, others would join in singing that same song.

10. Roberts, *Francis Schaeffer*, 100.

11. Schaeffer, *God Who Is There*, 175.

12. Ashford, *Every Square Inch*, 4.

13. Schaeffer, *True Spirituality*, 196.

Conclusion

Although not every apologetic approach can answer all the various arguments and critiques against Christianity, nor the means of proving every fine detail of the faith, testing the truthfulness of belief systems at the level of worldview has strengths that other approaches do not have. This approach is becoming more popular as the worldview concept itself continues to gain traction in both religious and philosophical endeavors. As argued in the first chapter, this approach arose in response to the unique challenges placed against Christianity in modern times. As people have more exposure to the different belief systems espoused in religion and philosophy, it becomes critical to demonstrate that all worldviews cannot be true. This is done by showing them that there are ways to test the systems for their truthfulness. While several worldviews attempt to relativize the truth, it is essential to demonstrate that this relativism is a worldview with no logical coherence. The truth-tests of this worldview apologetic reveal why pluralism is not tenable (because it goes against the laws of noncontradiction and is therefore not coherent) and why relativism is not plausible (since it is self-defeating and not livable). Worldview apologetic truth-tests can show people why these worldviews and issues are problematic while at the same time exhibiting Christianity as the only reasonable alternative. Moreover, it is because of competing worldviews, pluralistic ideals, and relativistic thinking that apologetics as a discipline is not past its prime—reasoned, critical thinking is needed now more than ever. An apologetic that one merely lives without the addition of rational argument and evidence cannot convince someone that one worldview is truer than another. However, an apologetic that is argued but not lived cannot convince others that it makes any sort of difference.

While worldview is a somewhat recent tool in the hands of philosophers, it is as old as thought itself. What makes worldview the perfect sphere from which to perform the apologetic task is its inescapability. Everyone has a worldview—the question is if the worldview is true or not. While individual beliefs make up a worldview, it is the system itself as a whole that must stand or fall on its merits. The truth-tests expose the strengths and weaknesses of each. Moreover, because opponents often challenge Christianity as an entire system, it only makes sense that the way of defense would be from the scope of it being an entire system.

The underlying logic for worldview apologetics is abductive reasoning. Whether consciously or not, one takes the data of life and generates (or chooses) a hypothesis to make sense of the data. One finds or creates a worldview that makes sense of life. However, abductive reasoning is also a means of evaluation. The tests of truth help determine if the hypothesis/ worldview has sufficiently considered the available data and if the conclusions are epistemically sound. What makes this approach unique is that the epistemological theories of truth that have lasted the test of time and the scrutiny of critics are the basis for the testing criteria. Each of the three theories has particular strengths and weaknesses. Therefore, the tests based on those theories also have their own strengths and weaknesses. The individual tests themselves may not fully reveal the truth or falsehood of a system, but together they have a more substantial chance to expose worldviews for their reliability. When one scrutinizes the major tenets of a worldview under the microscope of logical coherency, empirical adequacy, and experiential relevancy, what is at the system's core becomes uncovered for all to see.

Since worldviews have beliefs to make sense out of every area of life, it is vital to focus on the critical life questions for the context of worldview testing. While touching on most of the key issues of life, the areas of origin, meaning, morality, and destiny are particularly sound areas to expose the strengths and weaknesses of worldviews. It is not necessarily that all other worldviews are entirely wrong in each of the beliefs they cling to. As the old adage goes, even a broken clock tells the correct time twice a day. Neither is the one true worldview ever perfectly followed. Even Christians must retain humility since no espouser of that faith ever holds a perfectly correct Christian worldview. However, when all the core beliefs are taken to the three tests, even if a small minority of worldview beliefs are proven false, the worldview itself is suspect enough for someone to consider changing their belief structure. Therefore, this approach is important not only in scholarly considerations of apologetics but also within Christianity in its mission of evangelism around the world—exposing false beliefs for what they are and ingratiating the gospel of the Lord and Savior Jesus Christ. I pray that people worldwide who hold to non-Christian worldviews will have the roofs blown off of their false hopes and dreams and will walk the bridge to the eternal life of joy and peace found only in Jesus Christ as espoused by the Christian worldview.

Bibliography

Abraham, William J. "Cumulative Case Arguments for Christian Theism." In *The Rationality of Religious Belief: Essays in Honour of Basil Mitchell*, edited by William J. Abraham and Steven W. Holtzer, 17–37. Oxford: Clarendon, 1987.

Adler, Jonathan E. "Testimony, Trust, Knowing." *The Journal of Philosophy* 91, no. 5 (1994) 264–75.

Aliseda, Atocha. *Abductive Reasoning: Logical Investigations into Discovery and Explanation*. Dordrecht, Netherlands: Springer, 2006.

———. "Mathematical Reasoning vs. Abductive Reasoning: A Structural Approach." *Synthese* 134, no. 1/2 (2003) 25–44.

Allen, Tommy. "Transcendental Argument: Contours of C.S. Lewis' Apologetic." *Premise* 4, no. 4 (December 1997).

Alston, William P. *A Realist Conception of Truth*. Ithaca, NY: Cornell University, 1996.

Anderson, Tawa J., W. Michael Clark, and David K. Naugle. *An Introduction to Christian Worldview: Pursuing God's Perspective in a Pluralistic World*. Downers Grove: IVP Academic, 2017.

Anselm. "Anselm's Proslogium (or, Discourse on the Existence of God)." In *The Major Works of Anselm of Canterbury*, translated by Sidney Norton Deane, 1–34. Chicago: Open Court, 1939.

Aquinas, Thomas. *Summa Theologica*. Translated by Fathers of the English Dominican Province. London: Burns, Oates, and Washbourne, 1921.

Ashford, Bruce Riley. *Every Square Inch: An Introduction to Cultural Engagement for Christians*. Bellingham, WA: Lexham, 2015.

Atkins, Peter. "The Limitless Power of Science." In *Nature's Imagination: The Frontiers of Scientific Vision*, edited by John Cornwell, 122–32. Oxford: Oxford University Press, 1995.

Augustine. "The City of God." In *St. Augustin's City of God and Christian Doctrine*, edited by Philip Schaff, 1–511. Vol. 2, *A Select Library of Nicene and Post-Nicene Fathers*. New York: The Christian Literature Company, 1888.

———. "Lectures or Tractates on the Gospel According to St. John." In *St. Augustine*, edited by Philip Schaff, 1–452. Vol. 7, *A Select Library of Nicene and Post-Nicene Fathers*. New York: The Christian Literature Company, 1888.

———. "Soliloquies". In *St. Augustine*, edited by Philip Schaff, 531–60. Vol. 7, *A Select Library of Nicene and Post-Nicene Fathers*. New York: The Christian Literature Company, 1888.

Ayer, Alfred Jules. *Language Truth & Logic*. Dover Books on Western Philosophy. New York: Dover, 1952.

Barth, Karl. *The Doctrine of the Word of God*. Edited by G. W. Bromiley and T. F. Torrance. Translated by G. T. Thomson and Harold Knight. Vol. 1, *Church Dogmatics*. London: T & T Clark, 1956.

Bartholomew, Craig G. *Contours of the Kuyperian Tradition: A Systematic Introduction*. Downers Grove: IVP Academic, 2017.

Becker, Hjördis. "From Weltanschauung to Livs-Anskuelse: Kierkegaard's Existential Philosophy." *Humana.Mente Journal of Philosophical Studies* 18 (2011) 1–18.

Behe, Michael J. *Darwin's Black Box: The Biochemical Challenge to Evolution*. 10th Anniversary Edition. Free Press, 2006.

———. "Evidence for Design at the Foundation of Life." In *Science and Evidence for Design in the Universe: Paper Presented at a Conference Sponsored by the Wethersfield Institute*, 113–28. San Francisco: Ignatius, 2000.

Berlinski, David. *The Devil's Delusion: Atheism and Its Scientific Pretensions*. 2nd ed. New York: Basic, 2009.

Bertrand, J. Mark. *Rethinking Worldview: Learning to Think, Live, and Speak in This World*. Wheaton: Crossway, 2007.

Bloesch, Donald G. *The Ground of Certainty: Toward an Evangelical Theology of Revelation*. Eugene, OR: Wipf & Stock, 2002.

Bratt, James D. *Abraham Kuyper: Modern Calvinist, Christian Democrat*. Grand Rapids: Eerdmans, 2013.

Brown, William. "Thinking Worldviewishly." *Cedarville Torch* 26, no. 1 (Spring 2004) 4–7, 12, 14–15.

Burson, Scott R., and Jerry L. Walls. *C. S. Lewis & Francis Schaeffer: Lessons for a New Century from the Most Influential Apologists of Our Time*. Downers Grove: InterVarsity, 1998.

Butler, Joseph. *The Analogy of Religion: Natural and Revealed to the Constitution and Course of Nature*. Oxford: Clarendon, 1897.

Cabal, Ted. "The Worldview Concept as Evangelical Tool." In *48th National Conference— Jackson, MS*. Portland: Theological Research Exchange Network, 1996.

Carattini, Jill. "The Unstoppable Story." *Just Thinking Magazine*, May 25, 2017. https://rzim.org/just-thinking/the-unstoppable-story-jt-25-23/.

Carley, Kathleen. "A Theory of Group Stability." *American Sociological Review* 56, no. 3 (1991): 331–54.

Chan, Sewell. "Hitchens Debates Rabbi Wolpe on God." *New York Times*, November 3, 2008. https://cityroom.blogs.nytimes.com/2008/11/03/hitchens-vs-rabbi-on-god/comment-page-6/.

Chrysostom, John. "Demonstration against the Pagans That Christ Is God." In *Saint John Chrysostom: Apologist*, translated by Margaret A. Schatkin and Paul W. Harkins, 153–262. Vol. 73, *Fathers of the Church: A New Translation*. Washington, D.C.: The Catholic University of America Press, 1985.

Ciampolini, Anna, and Paolo Torroni. "Using Abductive Logic Agents for Modeling the Judicial Evaluation of Criminal Evidence." *Applied Artificial Intelligence* 18 (2004): 251–76.

Clark, Gordon H. *A Christian View of Men and Things.* Grand Rapids: Eerdmans, 1952.

Clark, W. Michael. "Islam: A Challenge to Our Missional Resolve." *The Southern Baptist Journal of Missions and Evangelism* 1, no. 1 (Summer 2012): 22–30.

Cohen, Michael. "Induction." In *The Oxford Companion to Philosophy*, edited by Ted Honderich, 405–6. Oxford: Oxford University Press, 1995.

Cole, Graham A. "Do Christians Have a Worldview?" Deerfield, IL: The Christ on Campus Initiative—Carl F. H. Henry Center for Theological Understanding, 2007.

Copleston, Frederick, and Bertrand Russell. "Debate on the Existence of God." BBC Radio, 1948. http://www.biblicalcatholic.com/apologetics/p20.htm.

Coppenger, Mark. *Moral Apologetics for Contemporary Christians: Pushing Back against Cultural and Religious Critics.* Nashville: B & H Academic, 2011.

Corduan, Winfried. *No Doubt about It: The Case for Christianity.* Nashville: Broadman & Holman Publishers, 1997.

———. *A Tapestry of Faiths: The Common Threads between Christianity & World Religions.* Downers Grove: InterVarsity, 2002.

Cotham, Perry C. *One World, Many Neighbors: A Christian Perspective on Worldviews.* Abilene, TX: Abilene Christian University Press, 2008.

Covington, David A. *A Redemptive Theology of Art: Restoring Godly Aesthetics to Doctrine and Culture.* Grand Rapids: Zondervan, 2018.

Craig, William Lane. *Reasonable Faith: Christian Truth and Apologetics.* 3rd ed. Wheaton: Crossway, 2008.

Crick, Francis. *Life Itself: Its Origin and Nature.* New York: Simon & Schuster, 1981.

Damer, T. Edward. *Attacking Faulty Reasoning.* 2nd ed. Belmont, CA: Wadsworth, 1987.

Darwin, Charles. *The Origin of Species by Means of Natural Selection.* 2nd ed. Vol. 49, *Great Books of the Western World.* Chicago: Encyclopaedia Britannica, 1990.

Darwish, Nonie. *Cruel and Unusual Punishment: The Terrifying Global Implications of Islamic Law.* Nashville: Thomas Nelson, 2008.

Davidson, Donald. "A Coherence Theory of Truth and Knowledge." In *Subjective, Intersubjective, Objective*, 137–57. Oxford: Clarendon, 2001.

Dewey, John. *Reconstruction in Philosophy.* New York: Henry Holt and Company, 1920.

Dooyeweerd, Herman. *A New Critique of Theoretical Thought.* Translated by David H. Freeman and William S. Young. Vol. 1, *The Necessary Presuppositions of Philosophy.* Jordan Station, Ontario: Paideia, 1984.

Douven, Igor. "Abduction." In *The Stanford Encyclopedia of Philosophy*, edited by Edward N. Zalta. 2011. http://plato.stanford.edu/archives/spr2011/entries/abduction/.

Dulles, Avery Cardinal. "The Deist Minimum." *First Things: A Monthly Journal of Religion and Public Life*, no. 149 (January 2005): 25–30.

———. *A History of Apologetics.* San Francisco: Ignatius, 1999.

Edgar, William, and K. Scott Oliphint, eds. *Christian Apologetics Past and Present: A Primary Source Reader.* 2 Vols. Wheaton: Crossway, 2009.

Ermarth, Michael. *Wilhelm Dilthey: The Critique of Historical Reason.* Chicago: University of Chicago Press, 1978.

Evans, A. Steven. "Matters of the Heart: Orality, Story and Cultural Transformation—The Critical Role of Storytelling in Affecting Worldview." *Missiology: An International Review* 38, no. 2 (April 2010): 185–99.

Bibliography

Fann, K. T. *Peirce's Theory of Abduction*. The Hague, Holland: Martinus Nijhoff, 1970.

Federer, William J., ed. *Great Quotations*. St. Louis, MO: AmeriSearch, 2001.

Feinburg, John S. *Can You Believe It's True?: Christian Apologetics in a Modern and Postmodern Era*. Wheaton: Crossway, 2013.

Feinburg, Paul D. "Cumulative Case Apologetics." In *Five Views on Apologetics*, edited by Steven B. Cowan, 147–72. Grand Rapids: Zondervan, 2000.

Fesko, J. V. "N. T. Wright on Prolgegomena." *Themelios* 31, no. 3 (April 2006): 6–31.

Flew, Antony. *God & Philosophy*. New York: Harcourt, Brace & World, Inc., 1966.

———. *There Is a God: How the World's Most Notorious Atheist Changed His Mind*. New York: HarperOne, 2007.

Forrest, Benjamin K., Joshua D. Chatraw, and Alister E. McGrath. *The History of Apologetics: A Biographical and Methodological Introduction*. Grand Rapids: Zondervan Academic, 2020.

Frame, John M.. *Apologetics to the Glory of God: An Introduction*. Phillipsburg, N.J.: Presbyterian and Reformed, 1994.

———. *The Doctrine of the Knowledge of God*. Phillipsburg, NJ: Presbyterian and Reformed, 1987.

———. *A History of Western Philosophy and Theology*. Phillipsburg, NJ: Presbyterian and Reformed, 2015.

Frankfurt, Harry G. "Peirce's Notion of Abduction." *The Journal of Philosophy* 55, no. 14 (1958): 593–97.

Frankl, Viktor E. *The Doctor and the Soul: From Psychotherapy to Logotherapy*. Translated by Richard Winston and Clara Winston. 2nd ed. New York: Vintage, 1986.

Geisler, Norman L. *Christian Apologetics*. 1st ed. Grand Rapids: Baker Book House, 1976.

———. *Christian Apologetics*. 2nd ed. Grand Rapids: Baker Academic, 2013.

Geisler, Norman L., and Ronald M. Brooks. *Come, Let Us Reason: An Introduction to Logical Thinking*. Grand Rapids: Baker Book House, 1990.

Geisler, Norman L., and William D. Watkins. *Worlds Apart: A Handbook on World Views*. 2nd ed. Grand Rapids: Baker Book House, 1989.

Geivett, R. Douglas. "David Hume and a Cumulative Case Argument." In *In Defense of Natural Theology: A Post-Humean Assessment*, edited by James F. Sennett and Douglas Groothuis, 297–329. Downers Grove: InterVarsity, 2005.

Goheen, Michael W., and Craig G. Bartholomew. *Living at the Crossroads: An Introduction to Christian Worldview*. Grand Rapids: Baker Academic, 2008.

Goldman, Steven. "The Psychology of Worldviews: Jaspers/Heidegger." *Presencing EPIS* 1, no. 1 (2012): 28–51.

Grant, Peter J. "The Priority of Apologetics in the Church." In *Is Your Church Ready?: Motivating Leaders to Live an Apologetic Life*, edited by Ravi Zacharias and Norman Geisler, 55–71. Grand Rapids: Zondervan, 2003.

Green, David W., and Rachel McCloy. "Reaching a Verdict." *Thinking & Reasoning* 9, no. 4 (2003): 307–33.

Grenier, Richard. *The Gandhi Nobody Knows*. Nashville: Thomas Nelson, 1983.

Groothuis, Douglas. *Christian Apologetics: A Comprehensive Case for Biblical Faith*. Downers Grove: InterVarsity, 2011.

———. "Jesus: Philosopher and Apologist." *Christian Research Journal* 25, no. 2 (2002). http://www.equip.org/article/jesus-philosopher-and-apologist/.

Guinness, Os. *Time for Truth: Living Free in a World of Lies, Hype & Spin*. Grand Rapids: Baker, 2000.

———. "Turning the Tables." *Just Thinking Magazine*, July 1, 2015. https://rzim.org/just-thinking/turning-the-tables/.

Habermas, Gary R. *The Historical Jesus: Ancient Evidence for the Life of Jesus.* Joplin, MO: College Press, 1996.

Habermas, Gary R., and Michael R. Licona. *The Case for the Resurrection of Jesus.* Grand Rapids: Kregel Publication, 2004.

Haikola, Lars. "Science, Religion and the Need for a World-View." *HTS Teologiese Studies/Theological Studies* 59, no. 3 (2003): 763–77.

Halas, Matus. "In Error We Trust: An Apology of Abductive Inference." *Cambridge Review of International Affairs* 28, no. 4 (2015): 701–20.

Harris, Sam. *The End of Faith: Religion, Terror, and the Future of Reason.* New York: W. W. Norton & Company, 2004.

Hasker, William. *Metaphysics: Constructing a World View.* Contours of Christian Philosophy. Downers Grove: InterVarsity, 1983.

Herbert, Edward. *The Antient Religion of the Gentiles and Causes of Their Errors Considered.* London, 1705.

Herms, Eilert. "'Weltanschaunng' Bei Friedrich Schleiermacher Und Albrecht Ritschl." In *Theorie Fur Die Praxis*, 121–43. Munich: Chr. Kaiser, 1982.

Heslam, Peter. *Creating a Christian Worldview: Abraham Kuyper's Lectures on Calvinism.* Grand Rapids: Eerdmans, 1998.

Hiebert, Paul G. *Transforming Worldviews: An Anthropological Understanding of How People Change.* Grand Rapids: Baker Academic, 2008.

Hitchens, Christopher. *God Is Not Great: How Religion Poisons Everything.* New York: Twelve, 2007.

Hoffmann, Michael. "Problems with Peirce's Concept of Abduction." *Foundations of Science* 4, no. 3 (1999): 271–305.

Holmes, Arthur F. *Contours of a World View.* Grand Rapids: Eerdmans, 1983.

Hookway, C. J. "Abduction." In *The Oxford Companion to Philosophy*, edited by Ted Honderich, 1. Oxford: Oxford University Press, 1995.

Hoover, Arlie J. *Dear Agnos: A Defense of Christianity.* Grand Rapids: Baker Book House, 1976.

Hoyle, Fred, and Chandra Wickramasinghe. *Evolution from Space: A Theory of Cosmic Creationism.* New York: Simon & Schuster, 1981.

Hume, David. *An Enquiry Concerning Human Understanding and Selections from a Treatise of Human Nature.* Chicago: Open Court, 1921.

Husserl, Edmund. "Philosophy as Rigorous Science." In *The New Yearbook for Phenomenology and Phenomenological Philosophy II*, edited by Burt Hopkins and Steven Crowell, translated by Marcus Brainard, II:249–95. London: Routledge, 2002.

"Inference." In *The Oxford Companion to Philosophy*, edited by Ted Honderich, 407. Oxford: Oxford University Press, 1995.

Irenaeus. "Against Heresies." In *The Ante-Nicene Fathers*, edited by Alexander Roberts and James Donaldson, 315–567. Vol. 1. Buffalo: The Christian Literature Company, 1885.

James, William. *Pragmatism: A New Name for Some Old Ways of Thinking.* Reprint. New York: Longmans, Green and Co., 1922.

Jastrow, Robert. *God and the Astronomers.* 2nd ed. New York: W. W. Norton & Company, 1992.

Johnson, Phillip E. "Nihilism and the End of Law." *First Things: A Monthly Journal of Religion and Public Life* 31 (March 1993): 19–25.

Bibliography

Jones, W. T. "World Views: Their Nature and Their Function." *Current Anthropology* 13, no. 1 (February 1972): 79–109.

Josephson, John R., and Susan G. Josephson. *Abductive Inference: Computation, Philosophy, Technology*. Cambridge: Cambridge University Press, 1996.

Josephus, Flavius. *The Antiquities of the Jews*. Translated by William Whiston. The Works of Josephus. Peabody, MA: Hendrickson, 1987.

Kahane, Howard. *Logic and Contemporary Rhetoric: The Use of Reason in Everyday Life.* 5th ed. Belmont, CA: Wadsworth, 1988.

Kant, Immanuel. *Critique of Judgment: Including the First Introduction.* Translated by Werner S. Pluhar. Indianapolis: Hackett, 1987.

Khachab, Chihab El. "The Logical Goodness of Abduction in C. S. Peirce's Thought." *Transactions of the Charles S. Peirce Society* 49, no. 2 (2013): 157–77.

Kierkegaard, Søren. "Af En Endu Levendes Papirer," 1838.

Kuipers, Theo A. F. "Naive and Refined Truth Approximation." *Synthese* 93, no. 3 (1992): 299–341.

Kumar, K. Suresh. "Humanism Philosophy." *Global Journal for Research Analysis* 6, no. 9 (September 2017): 81–82.

Kuyper, Abraham. *Calvinism: Six Lectures Delivered in the Theological Seminary at Princeton*. New York: Fleming H. Revell, 1899.

Lecky, W. E. H. *History of European Morals from Augustus to Charlemagne*. New York: D. Appleton & Co., 1903.

Leff, Arthur Allen. "Unspeakable Ethics, Unnatural Law." *Duke Law Journal* 1979, no. 6 (December 1979): 1229–49.

Lewis, C. S. *Miracles: A Preliminary Study*. Revised. New York: HarperOne, 1960.

Lewis, Clarence Irving. *Mind and the World-Order*. New York: Dover, 1929.

Lewontin, Richard. "Billions and Billions of Demons." *The New York Review of Books*, January 9, 1997.

Litfin, Bryan A. "Tertullian of Carthage: African Apologetics Enters the Fray." In *The History of Apologetics: A Biographical and Methodological Introduction*, edited by Benjamin K. Forrest, Joshua D. Chatraw, and Alister E. McGrath, 85–101. Grand Rapids: Zondervan Academic, 2020.

Long, Jimmy. "The Undeniable Depravity of the Human Heart and Our Hope in Jesus Christ." *Be Transformed.* https://jimmylong.net/2013/11/23/the-undeniable-depravity-of-the-human-heart/

Luther, Martin. *Concerning Christian Liberty*. Vol. 36. Harvard Classics. New York: P F Collier & Son, 1917.

MacIntyre, Alasdair. *Difficulties in Christian Belief*. New York: Philosophical Library, 1959.

Mackie, J. L. "Evil and Omnipotence." *Mind* 64, no. 254 (April 1955): 200–212.

Magnani, Lorenzo. "Abduction and Chance Discovery in Science." *International Journal of Knowledge-Based and Intelligent Engineering Systems* 11 (2007): 273–79.

Markos, Louis. "Debating Design—Letter to Journal." *First Things* 242 (April 2014): 10–11.

Marlow, A. R., ed. "Proceedings of the Third Loyola Conference on Quantum Theory and Gravitation." *International Journal of Theoretical Physics* 25, no. 5–6 (1986): 465–661.

Martyr, Justin. "First Apology." In *The Ante-Nicene Fathers*, edited by Alexander Roberts and James Donaldson, 163–87. Vol. 1. Buffalo, NY: The Christian Literature Company, 1885.

McAllister, Stuart, *Truth and Reality*. Foundations of Apologetics. Ravi Zacharias International Ministries. https://www.rightnowmedia.org/Content/Series/161813?episode=2.

Bibliography

McCarthy, Vincent A. *The Phenomenology of Moods in Kierkegaard*. Boston: Martinus Nijhoff, 1978.

McDowell, Sean. "Was Jesus an Apologist?" *Sean McDowell Blog* (blog), September 26, 2017. https://seanmcdowell.org/blog/was-jesus-an-apologist.

McGoldrick, James Edward. "Claiming Every Inch: The Worldview of Abraham Kuyper." In *A Christian Worldview: Essays from a Reformed Perspective*, edited by C. N. Willborn, 31–46. Taylors, SC: Presbyterian, 2008.

McKaughan, Daniel J. "From Ugly Duckling to Swan: C. S. Peirce, Abduction, and the Pursuit of Scientific Theories." *Transactions of the Charles S. Peirce Society* 44, no. 3 (2008): 446–68.

McLellan, Alex. *A Jigsaw Guide to Making Sense of the World*. Downers Grove: Intervarsity Press, 2012.

Mill, John Stuart. *Utilitarianism*. 7th ed. London: Longmans, Green and Co., 1879.

Mirza, Noeman A, Noori Akhtar-Danesh, Charlotte Noesgaard, Lynn Martin, and Eric Staples. "A Concept Analysis of Abductive Reasoning." *Journal of Advanced Nursing* 70, no. 9 (2014): 1980–94.

Mitchell, Basil. *The Justification of Religious Belief*. London: MacMillan, 1973.

Montgomery, John Warwick. "A Short History of Apologetics." In *Christian Apologetics: An Anthology of Primary Sources*, edited by Khaldoun A. Sweis and Chad V. Meister, 21–28. Grand Rapids: Zondervan, 2012.

Moreau, A. Scott. "Paul G. Hiebert's Legacy of Worldview." *Trinity Journal* 30, no. 2 (Fall 2009): 223–33.

Moreland, J. P., and William Lane Craig. *Philosophical Foundations for a Christian Worldview*. 2nd ed. Downers Grove: IVP Academic, 2017.

Mouw, Richard J. *Abraham Kuyper: A Short and Personal Introduction*. Grand Rapids: Eerdmans, 2011.

Murray, Abdu. "Aspiring Angels." *Just Thinking Magazine*, February 23, 2017. https://rzim.org/just-thinking/aspiring-angels/.

————. "Islam or Christianity: Reflections on God's Greatness." *Just Thinking Magazine*, December 14, 2015. https://rzim.org/just-thinking/islam-or-christianity-reflections-on-gods-greatness/.

Nash, Ronald H. *Life's Ultimate Questions: An Introduction to Philosophy*. Grand Rapids: Zondervan, 1999.

————. *Worldviews in Conflict: Choosing Christianity in a World of Ideas*. Grand Rapids: Zondervan, 1992.

Naugle, David K. "Wilhelm Dilthey's Doctrine of World Views and Its Relationship to Hermeneutics." Arlington, TX: University of Texas at Arlington, Spring 1993. http://www3.dbu.edu/naugle/pdf/wilhelm_dilthey.pdf.

————. *Worldview: The History of a Concept*. Grand Rapids: Eerdmans, 2002.

Netland, Harold A. *Christianity & Religious Diversity: Clarifying Christian Commitments in a Globalizing Age*. Grand Rapids: Baker Academic, 2015.

————. *Dissonant Voices: Religious Pluralism and the Question of Truth*. Vancouver: Regent College, 1991.

————. *Encountering Religious Pluralism: The Challenge to Christian Faith & Mission*. Downers Grove: IVP Academic, 2001.

Nielsen, Kai. "Why Should I Be Moral? Revisited." *American Philosophical Quarterly* 21, no. 1 (January 1984): 81–91.

Nietzsche, Friedrich. *Twilight of the Idols*. Translated by Richard Polt. Indianapolis: Hackett, 1997.

Noebel, David. *The Battle for Truth: Defending the Christian Worldview in the Marketplace of Ideas*. Eugene, OR: Harvest House, 2001.

O'Brien, Dan. *An Introduction to the Theory of Knowledge*. 2nd ed. Cambridge: Polity, 2017.

Okasha, Samir. "Van Fraassen's Critique of Inference to the Best Explanation." *Studies in History and Philosophy of Science* 31, no. 4 (2000): 691–710.

Oliphint, K. Scott. "The Reformed World View." In *A Christian Worldview: Essays from a Reformed Perspective*, edited by C. N. Willborn, 1–30. Taylors, SC: Presbyterian, 2008.

Orr, James. *The Christian View of God and the World: As Centring in the Incarnation*. 8th ed. New York: Charles Scribner's Sons, 1907.

Oxford Dictionary. "Word of the Year 2016 Is . . ." https://en.oxforddictionaries.com/word-of-the-year/word-of-the-year-2016.

Paley, William. *Natural Theology*. Vol. 1, *The Works of William Paley*. London: Longman and Company, 1838.

Parrot, Justin. *Reconciling the Divine Decree and Free Will in Islam*. Irving, TX: Yaqeen Institute for Islamic Research, 2017.

Payne, Thomas. *The Age of Reason: Being an Investigation of True and of Fabulous Theology*. Boston: Thomas Hall, 1794.

Peirce, Charles Sanders. *Collected Papers of Charles Sanders Peirce*. Edited by Charles Hartshorne and Paul Weiss. 8 vols. Cambridge, MA: Belknap, 1931–1958.

Penner, Myron Bradley. *The End of Apologetics: Christian Witness in a Postmodern Context*. Kindle. Grand Rapids: Baker Academic, 2013.

Plantinga, Alvin C.. "An Evolutionary Argument against Naturalism." *Religious and Theological Studies Fellowship Bulletin* 11 (April 1996): 9–14.

———. *God, Freedom, and Evil*. Grand Rapids: Eerdmans, 1974.

———. "Is Belief in God Properly Basic?" *Nous* 15, no. 1 (March 1981): 41–51.

———. "Reason and Belief in God." In *Faith and Rationality: Reason and Belief in God*, edited by Alvin Plantinga and Nicholas Wolterstorff, 16–93. Notre Dame: University of Notre Dame Press, 1983.

Poe, Harry L. *The Gospel and Its Meaning*. Grand Rapids: Zondervan, 1996.

Presley, Stephen O. "Irenaeus of Lyons: Anti-Gnostic Polemicist." In *The History of Apologetics: A Biographical and Methodological IntroductionG*, edited by Benjamin K. Forrest, Joshua D. Chatraw, and Alister E. McGrath, 49–66. Grand Rapids: Zondervan Academic, 2020.

Psillos, Stathis. "On Van Fraassen's Critique of Abductive Reasoning." *The Philosophical Quarterly* 46, no. 182 (1996): 31–47.

Quine, W. V. *Pursuit of Truth*. Cambridge, MA: Harvard University Press, 1990.

Rana, Fazale. *The Cell's Design: How Chemistry Reveals the Creator's Artistry*. Grand Rapids: Baker, 2008.

Rand, Ayn. "The Objectivist Ethics." 1964. https://campus.aynrand.org/works/1961/01/01/the-objectivist-ethics/page1.

Roberts, Mostyn. *Francis Schaeffer*. Darlington, England: Evangelical, 2012.

Russell, Bertrand. "A Free Man's Worship." In *Why I Am Not a Christian*. Philadelphia: The Great Library Collection, 2015.

———. "Letter to the 'Observer,'" October 6, 1957.

Samples, Kenneth Richard. *Without a Doubt: Answering the 20 Toughest Faith Questions*. Grand Rapids: Baker, 2004.

Bibliography

————. *A World of Difference: Putting Christian Truth-Claims to the Worldview Test.* Grand Rapids: Baker, 2007.

Schaeffer, Francis A. *The God Who Is There.* Vol. 1, *The Complete Works of Francis A. Schaeffer: A Christian Worldview.* Wheaton: Crossway, 1982.

————. *The Great Evangelical Disaster.* Vol. 4, *The Complete Works of Francis A. Schaeffer: A Christian Worldview.* Wheaton: Crossway, 1982.

————. *He Is There and He Is Not Silent.* Vol. 1, *The Complete Works of Francis A. Schaeffer: A Christian Worldview.* Wheaton: Crossway, 1982.

————. *How Should We Then Live?* Vol. 5, *The Complete Works of Francis A. Schaeffer: A Christian Worldview.* Wheaton: Crossway, 1982.

————. *True Spirituality.* Vol. 3, *The Complete Works of Francis A. Schaeffer: A Christian Worldview.* Wheaton: Crossway, 1982.

Schaeffer, Francis A., and C. Everett Koop. *Whatever Happened to the Human Race?* Vol. 5, *The Complete Works of Francis A. Schaeffer: A Christian Worldview.* Wheaton: Crossway, 1982.

Schleiermacher, Friedrich. *On Religion: Speeches to Its Cultured Despisers.* Translated by John Oman. London: Kegan Paul, Trench, Trubner and Company, 1893.

Schleifer, Ronald, and Jerry Vannatta. "The Logic of Diagnosis: Peirce, Literary Narrative, and the History of Present Illness." *The Journal of Medicine and Philosophy* 31, no. 4 (2006): 363–84.

Schultz, Katherine G., and James A. Swezey. "A Three-Dimensional Concept of Worldview." *Journal of Research on Christian Education* 22, no. 3 (2013): 227–43.

Scorgie, Glen G. *A Call for Continuity: The Theological Contribution of James Orr.* Macon, GA: Mercer University Press, 1988.

Sennett, James F. "Hume's Stopper and the Natural Theology Project." In *In Defense of Natural Theology: A Post-Humean Assessment,* edited by James F. Sennett and Douglas Groothuis, 82–104. Downers Grove: InterVarsity, 2005.

Shelley, Cameron. "Visual Abductive Reasoning in Archaeology." *Philosophy of Science* 63, no. 2 (1996): 278–301.

Sherman, Steven B. *Revitalizing Theological Epistemology: Holistic Evangelical Approaches to the Knowledge of God.* Princeton Theological Monograph Series 83. Eugene, OR: Pickwick, 2008.

Sims, Bryan Billard. "Evangelical Worldview Analysis: A Critical Assessment and Proposal." PhD diss., The Southern Baptist Theological Seminary, 2006.

Sire, James W. *Naming the Elephant: Worldview as a Concept.* 2nd ed. Downers Grove: IVP Academic, 2015.

————. *The Universe Next Door: A Basic Worldview Catalog.* 5th ed. Downers Grove: InterVarsity, 2009.

Solzhenitsyn, Aleksandr. "Men Have Forgotten God—The Templeton Address." London, 1983. http://www.pravoslavie.ru/47643.html.

Stewart, Robert. "N. T. Wright's Hermeneutic: An Exploration." *The Churchman* 117, no. 2 (2003): 153–68.

Story, Dan. *Christianity on the Offense: Responding to the Beliefs and Assumptions of Spiritual Seekers.* Grand Rapids: Kregel, 1998.

Sweetman, Brendan. "Lyotard, Postmodernism, and Religion." *Philosophia Christi* 7, no. 1 (2005): 139–51.

Swinburne, Richard. *The Existence of God.* 2nd ed. Oxford: Clarendon, 2004.

Tacitus. *The Annals.* 2nd ed. Vol. 14, *Great Books of the Western World.* Chicago: Encyclopaedia Britannica, 1990.

Tertullian. *The Apology.* In *The Ante-Nicene Fathers,* edited by Alexander Roberts and James Donaldson. Translated by S. Thelwall. Vol. 3. Buffalo: The Christian Literature Company, 1885.

Thagard, Paul. "Forward." In *Abduction, Reason, and Science: Processes of Discovery and Explanation,* by Lorenzo Magnani, ix. New York: Springer Science+Business Media, 2001.

Thiselton, A. C. "Truth." In *New International Dictionary of New Testament Theology,* edited by Colin Brown, 874–901. Grand Rapids: Zondervan, 1986.

Tinker, Melvin. "Reasonable Belief? Providing Some of the Groundwork for an Effective Christian Apologetic." *The Churchman* 125, no. 4 (2011): 343–58.

Tuzet, Giovanni. "Legal Abduction." *Cognitio* 6, no. 2 (2005): 41–49.

van Fraassen, Bas C. *Laws and Symmetry.* Oxford: Clarendon, 1989.

———. *The Scientific Image.* Clarendon Library of Logic and Philosophy. Oxford: Clarendon, 1980.

Van Til, Cornelius. *The Defense of the Faith.* Philadelphia: Presbyterian and Reformed, 1955.

Vidal, Clement. "What Is a Worldview? {Wat Is Een Wereldbeeld?}." In *Nieuwheid Denken. De Wetenschappen En Het Creatieve Aspect van de Werkelijkheid.,* edited by H. Van Belle and J. Van der Veken. Leuven: Acco, 2008.

Vitale, Vince. "Pluralism." In *Jesus Among Secular Gods: The Countercultural Claims of Christ,* edited by Ravi Zacharias and Vince Vitale, 93–136. New York: FaithWords, 2017.

———. "Scientism." In *Jesus Among Secular Gods: The Countercultural Claims of Christ,* edited by Ravi Zacharias and Vince Vitale, 63–92. New York: FaithWords, 2017.

———. "The Trajectory of Truth." *Just Thinking Magazine,* February 23, 2017. https://rzim.org/just-thinking/the-trajectory-of-truth/.

Wainwright, William J. *Philosophy of Religion.* Belmont, CA: Wadsworth, 1988.

———. "Worldviews, Criteria and Epistemic Circularity." In *Inter-Religious Models and Criteria,* edited by J. Kellenberger, 87–105. New York: St. Martin's, 1993.

Walker, Ralph C. S. "The Coherence Theory." In *The Nature of Truth: Classic and Contemporary Perspectives,* edited by Michael P. Lynch, 123–58. Cambridge, MA: Massachusetts Institute of Technology, 2001.

Wallace, J. Warner. *Cold-Case Christianity: A Homicide Detective Investigates the Claims of the Gospels.* Colorado Springs: David C. Cook, 2013.

Walsh, Brian J., and J. Richard Middleton. *The Transforming Vision: Shaping a Christian Worldview.* Downers Grove: InterVarsity, 1984.

Walton, Douglas. *Abductive Reasoning.* Tuscaloosa, AL: The University of Alabama Press, 2005.

Walton, Douglas N. *Informal Logic: A Handbook for Critical Argumentation.* Cambridge: Cambridge University Press, 1989.

Ward, Jr., Mark L., Brian Collins, Bryan Smith, Gregory Stiekes, and Dennis Cone. *Biblical Worldview: Creation, Fall, Redemption.* Greenville, SC: BJU Press, 2016.

Warfield, Benjamin Breckinridge. *Revelation and Inspiration.* Vol. 1, *The Works of Benjamin B Warfield.* Grand Rapids: Baker Book House, 1932.

Wellum, Stephen. "Ideas Have Consequences: Lessons from the Theology of Francis Schaeffer." *Credo* 2, no. 5 (October 2012): 43–55.

Bibliography

White, Alan R. *Truth.* London: MacMillan, 1970.

Wilson, Douglas. *The Paideia of God and Other Essays on Education.* Moscos, ID: Canon Press, 1999.

Wittgenstein, Ludwig. *Tractatus Logico-Philosophicus.* 8th impression. London: Routledge & Kegan Paul, 1960.

Wolters, Albert M. *Creation Regained: Biblical Basics for a Reformational Worldview.* 2nd ed. Grand Rapids: Eerdmans, 2005.

————. "On the Idea of Worldview and Its Relation to Philosophy." In *Stained Glass: Worldviews and Social Science,* edited by Paul A. Marshall, Sander Griffioen, and Richard J. Mouw, 14–25. Lanham, MD: University Press of America, 1989.

Wright, N. T. *The New Testament and the People of God.* Vol. 1, *Christian Origins and the Question of God.* London: Society for Promoting Christian Knowledge, 1992.

Zwemer, Samuel M. *The Moslem Doctrine of God: An Essay on the Character and Attributes of Allah According to the Koran and Orthodox Tradition.* New York: American Tract Society, 1905.

Made in the USA
Columbia, SC
05 December 2024

48544740R00100